TRAGIC DRAMA

IN

AESCHYLUS, SOPHOCLES, AND SHAKESPEARE

AN ESSAY

TRAGIC DRAMA

IN

AESCHYLUS, SOPHOCLES, AND SHAKESPEARE

AN ESSAY

BY

LEWIS CAMPBELL, M.A., LL.D., D.LITT.

Senectuti seposui

NEW YORK
RUSSELL & RUSSELL · INC
1965

7621

FIRST PUBLISHED IN 1904

REISSUED, 1965, BY RUSSELL & RUSSELL, INC.

L.C. CATALOG CARD NO: 65—13953

PRINTED IN THE UNITED STATES OF AMERICA

PREFACE

IT was said of Goldsmith that he would travel to Kamschatka and bring back a wheelbarrow as a novelty. I am prepared to hear that much in this volume is unoriginal and has been better said elsewhere. For my reading in the literature of the subject has been casual and fragmentary. But my object has been to give expression to some thoughts which have long haunted and troubled me. The result may be a poor thing, but it is my own.

My love for Shakespeare dates from 1838, when my poet-cousin presented me with the copy of his edition which I still possess. I have revered Aeschylus since 1847, when I read the 'Prometheus' for the first time at school; and in the following year I improved my acquaintance with Sophocles by reading the seven plays without assistance for the Greek Blackstone prize at Glasgow. Ταῦτα μὲν οὖν᾽ μνήμῃ κεχαρίσθω.

It may seem strange to have omitted Euripides from a survey such as is here attempted, and he has certainly many affinities with Shakespeare. But his work seems more akin to the romantic drama of the Elizabethan and Jacobean periods than to the tragic masterpieces. I leave this hint to be developed by some one who is more intimate with 'Euripides the human' than I profess to be.

On some minute questions of interpretation and criticism, I have ventured to dissent from the high authority of Sir Richard Jebb. I 'join with all the world' in admiring the accuracy, brilliance, and completeness of his edition of Sophocles. But it will not surprise him that a former editor should not accept his judgment on every detail. Τὰ μὲν γὰρ πλεῖστα ἀμέμπτως ἐποίησε· χαλεπὸν δ' ἴσως πάντα.

In treating separately of the general subject, and of the several authors and their tragic dramas in particular, it was difficult to avoid some repetition. I trust to the reader's generosity to look indulgently on this and other imperfections.

Some portions of the present Essay have previously appeared in the 'Fortnightly' and 'National' Reviews, the 'Journal of Philology' and the 'Hibbert Journal.' My best acknowledgments are due to the proprietors and editors of these periodicals for the permission to republish which they have so readily accorded to me.

LEWIS CAMPBELL.

CONTENTS

CHAPTER VIII

TRAGIC DICTION (*continued*)

PART II

CHAPTER IX

AESCHYLUS

CHAPTER X

SOPHOCLES

CHAPTER XI

THE GROWTH OF SERIOUSNESS IN SHAKESPEARE

CHAPTER XVI

' CYMBELINE,' ' WINTER'S TALE,' AND ' TEMPEST '

PART I.

CHAPTER I

INTRODUCTORY

Scope of the work, how limited and why—Ancient and Modern Tragedy, different, yet analogous—Prevalent opinions, old and new—Dionysiac and Apolline elements—Links of connection between the ancient and modern—Shakespearian tragedy an independent growth—The Age of Tragedy.

I DO not seek for a new definition of tragedy, nor shall I proceed through an examination of the 'Poetics' of Aristotle, though no treatment of the subject can be independent of his theory. The purpose of this volume is to invite attention to some essential points of correspondence between the great masterpieces of Athens and of Elizabethan England. These resemblances are apt to be obscured by the differences of origin and of surroundings which inevitably separate from one another the productions of peoples so remote in place and time. But in so far as the analogy is real, it is the more remarkable because of the diversity.

Mr. Churton Collins, whose acute perception of similarities in literature is perhaps unrivalled, has lately argued with much plausibility for the unfamiliar thesis that Shakespeare had read the Greek

Tragedies, at least in Latin translations. That
Shakespeare could read Latin and was acquainted
with Ovid, for example, at first hand, had already
been made probable by several writers, especially by
the late Professor Thomas Spencer Baynes in his
' Shakespeare Studies ' ; and mention has been made
of an early English version of the ' Antigone.' But
that our poet's knowledge of the ancient dramas
extended beyond ' Seneca read by candle-light '
appears to me very difficult to prove. Mr. Collins,
however, concludes his essay with some words
in which I can heartily agree. ' Such an inquiry is
surely not without interest or even without importance. It shows how little the essential truths of
life and nature are affected by the accidents of time
and place. It reveals the kinship between men of
genius, separated by more than two thousand years,
and working under conditions which have nothing
in common, as well as the kinship between ancient
and modern art.' And, as will appear presently, I
am far from saying that there is no link of affiliation
between the modern and the ancient forms, although
I maintain that our national drama was directly
evolved from native antecedents, however indirectly
modified through the interest which the Renaissance
had awakened in the glories of antiquity.

The main differences between the Attic and the
Elizabethan theatres may be briefly stated at the
outset.

(1) *Simplicity and Complexity.*—In one sense
the ancient drama is more complex ; for it was the
meeting point of all the arts affecting ear or eye :
the outcome of song and dance, of epic recitation, of
statuesque grouping, of rhetorical argument, and of
religious presentation, blended in one harmonious
result. M. E. Faguet has observed that in different
modern nations these factors have been separately
cultivated : in Italy the musical, spectacular, and
orchestic, in France the rhetorical, in England the
poetic and the purely dramatic. The masque and
the opera have in our country been distinct develop-
ments, less rooted in the life of the nation. Such
rude scenic properties as existed in the earlier time
were mostly reserved for the pageant or the mystery
play. The masque, with its elaborate machinery,
was an aristocratic and royal luxury ; and the
accompaniments of music and scenery were for the
first time added after the closing of the theatres,
when Sir William Davenant, returning from France,
produced in 'The Siege of Rhodes' a public enter-
tainment supposed to be different in kind from
the popular drama, and therefore exempt from the
censures of Puritan authority.

But when considered merely as drama the ancient
form is, of course, more simple. In Sophocles
especially the action of each play is concentrated
in one critical point. After a brief exposition of
the antecedents there is a rapid climax, and the

culmination of interest is followed by an immediate
sequel.   Shakespeare works on larger lines, in this
more resembling Aeschylus, whose trilogies dealt
with successive acts of one great fable.

(2) *Objectivity and Subjectivity.*—It is a commonplace of philosophy that ancient modes of regarding
life are objective and that modern reflection becomes
increasingly subjective.   Accordingly in the Greek
drama the action as such is more prominent than
the development of character.   But this difference
is by no means absolute.   In the Shakespearian
masterpieces, the action, resulting from the interplay
of situation and character, becomes more and more
distinctly shaped into a solid and consistent whole;
while on the Attic stage the persons, who in the
traditional fable had been the passive victims of
destiny, are presented with more and more definite-
ness of characterisation and fineness of psychological
delineation; there is a gradual advance from such
broad outlines as in the figures of Atossa and Eteocles to the elaborate contrast between Neoptolemus
and Philoctetes.   Sophocles anticipated the truth, so
amply illustrated by Shakespeare, that character and
fate are one; and in Shakespeare as in Sophocles
the limitations surrounding the highest efforts of the
human will are acknowledged as a lesson of experience.   It follows from the attribute of simplicity
that the ancient dramatist presents his persons in a
few bold strokes and with a massiveness that is alien

from the modern stage ; but to say that Clytemnestra, Ajax, Deianira, Philoctetes, are types only
and not individual personalities, is surely an exaggeration.

(3) *Realism and Idealism.*—The demand of the
Elizabethan public was for bustling business on
the stage. They required that the story should be
presented in action, not merely represented to the
mind. Hence arose a superficial contrast which
detracts something from the perfection and due
proportion even of Shakespeare's art. The murder
of Banquo and the putting out of Gloster's eyes
are extreme instances. But the essential movement
of the Shakespearian drama is not the less ideal.
The impression left upon the mind of a competent
spectator by the action of 'Hamlet' or 'Othello' is that
of a great masterpiece, in which one whole aspect
of the life of man is summed up and typified—the
more completely because every detail is so true to
actual life.

(4) *Concentration and Comprehensiveness.*—From
what was said under the heading of simplicity it
follows that the ancient drama was marked by concentration ; the modern rather by comprehensiveness. But in the great masterpieces of the modern
as of the ancient stage, there is, notwithstanding,
an essential unity of impression and of interest.
Mr. Richard Moulton well observes : [1] ' The print of

[1] *Shakespeare as a Dramatic Artist*, p. 252.

modern life is marked by its comprehensiveness and
reconciliation of opposites; and nothing is more important in dramatic history than the way in which
Shakespeare and his contemporaries created a new
department in art, by seizing upon the rude jumble
of sport and earnest which the mob loved, and
converting it into a source of strong passion effect.
For a new faculty of mental grasp is generated
by this harmony of tones in the English drama;
the mixture of tones, so to speak, makes passion of
three dimensions.' 'Ancient tragedy clung to unity
of action and excluded such matter as threatened
to set up a second interest in a play. Modern
plot has a unity of a much more elaborate order—
a harmony of distinct actions each of which has
its separate unity.' [1] ' Shakespeare has elevated the
whole conception of plot from that of a mere unity
of action obtained by reduction of the amount of
matter presented, to that of a harmony of design
binding together concurrent actions from which no
degree of complexity was excluded.' [2]

(5) *The Comic Element.*—Attic drama made a
sharp distinction between tragedy and comedy. Yet
in the severest tragedies, as Horace observes, the art
retains traces of its rustic origin—*vestigia ruris.*
The Herald in the 'Supplices' of Aeschylus, the Nurse
in the ' Choephori,' the Watchman in the ' Antigone,'
the Phrygian slave in the ' Orestes,' are often quoted

---

[1] *Shakespeare as a Dramatic Artist,* p. 370.   [2] *Ib.* p. 286.

as examples of this. Even in the ' Oedipus Tyrannus,' that most severe of dramas, the crowning horror is evolved through a realistic contrast between a Corinthian peasant and a Theban slave.

Before proceeding further it may be well to present in one view some general notions about tragic drama which have prevailed in ancient and modern times.

Plato, because he feared that the excitement of the emotions, through a means so powerful and so hard to regulate, might unfit men for the rational conduct of their lives—although himself a poet—would have banished tragic poetry from his ideal state. Aristotle, on the other hand, whose philosophy aimed more at understanding the phenomena of human life than at transforming human nature, obtained a truer insight into the matter. The emotions cannot be suppressed, but they may be relieved of their grosser elements, they may be refined and elevated, through being called forth in sympathy with ideal sorrows apart from the pain and the confusion which attend them under the pressure of a real misfortune. The Greek philosopher's definition is thus translated by Professor Butcher:

' Tragedy is an imitation of an action, serious, complete, and of a certain magnitude ; in language embellished with each kind of ornament; the several kinds being found in separate parts of the play; in

the form of action, not of narrative; through pity
and fear effecting the proper *Katharsis*, or purgation
of these emotions.'

Milton in his preface to ' Samson Agonistes ' puts
it briefly thus : ' Tragedy hath been said by Aristotle
to be of power by raising pity and fear or terror, to
purge the mind of those and such-like passions, that
is to temper and reduce them to just measure with a
kind of delight, stirred up by reading or seeing those
passions well imitated.'　Dryden's paraphrase may
also be quoted here :

' Tragedy . . . is an imitation of one entire, great,
and probable action; not told, but represented,
which, by moving in us fear and pity, is conducive
to the purging of those two passions in our minds.'
(Preface to ' Troilus and Cressida.')

Dryden acknowledged that if Aristotle had been
acquainted with other dramas than the Greek, he
might have altered his definition.　And Aristotle himself expressed a doubt whether all possible forms of
tragic art had been developed.　Yet his definition can
never lose its value or its inexhaustible suggestiveness.

The contemplation of a grief that is not ours in
its beginning, middle, and end awakens pity and fear—
pity for another, and fear because we are also human; [1]

---

[1] Cf. Matthew Arnold's Notebooks, p. 7 (1858) :—' What is the
cause of this love for pain, in this modification of it ?　It is, says
St. Augustine, because *Jemand will zwar nicht leidend aber wohl*

while such distant contemplation of a distress not immediately afflicting us awakens thoughts bearing upon the whole of human life, which deepen our nature and render us more fit to encounter the changes and chances which may be in store for ourselves. Not those who are absorbed in the feeling of their own sorrows, but rather those who in the midst of prosperity or of business can yield for an hour or two to the contemplation of imaginary possibilities, find the keenest enjoyment at such a festival. And for those who live in the midst of petty cares, or are wearied with the monotony and insipidity of ordinary life, it is also good sometimes to be there. As Browning's Balaustion says :

> ' Small rebuked by large,
> We felt our puny hates refine to air,
> Our prides as poor prevent the humbling hand,
> Our petty passion purify its tide.'

Baron Bunsen, in his work on ' God in History,' regards the chief motive of ancient tragedy as the retribution following upon some exaggeration of self. But the spectator of a tragic drama is too much in sympathy with the hero to moralise about him like an indifferent bystander. He is not contemplating the situation from without, but entering into it heart and soul from within. ' Poetical justice ' is by no means indispensable to the highest tragedy. Else

mitleidend sein; and this desire springs *aus dem Quell hingebender Menschenliebe.*'

Dr. Johnson would have been justified, who in this respect appears to have preferred Massinger to Shakespeare.

The philosophers of the nineteenth century agreed with Aristotle in including a theory of aesthetics and of the principles of tragic poetry as a necessary factor in their systems. But their treatment of the art still reminds one of Plato's saying that 'there is an old quarrel between philosophy and poetry.' Each thinker climbs to his own pinnacle of speculation, from which many things that have an interest for other men seem 'small and indistinguishable, like far-off mountains turning into clouds.' Their sweeping generalisations omit particulars which are essential to the completeness of the art. Hegel, in generalising from the subject of the 'Antigone,' as he conceived it, spoke of tragedy as consisting in the conflict of opposing rights, which from a philosophical point of view are taken up or harmonised in a higher unity. But did any spectator, ancient or modern, so far sympathise with the Creon of the 'Antigone' as to think of him as acting within his rights? And were it granted for the sake of argument that this theory is applicable to the 'Antigone,' or to the 'Prometheus Bound,' it would have to be strained and forced if it were sought to apply it to the 'Oedipus,' or to the 'Medea.' No doubt there is a conflict or struggle of some kind preceding the determination of the event, but the attitude of the spectator is not that of a judge weighing opposite claims, but that of a friend whose sympathies are keenly enlisted for the chief person.

Goethe's confession in a letter to Zelter is characteristic : ' Ich bin nicht zum tragischen Dichter geboren, weil meine Natur conciliant ist ; daher kann der rein tragische Fall nicht interessiren, welcher eigentlich von Haus aus unversöhnlich sein muss ; und in dieser übrigens so äusserst platten Welt kommt mir das Unversöhnliche ganz absurd vor.' But is the subject of tragedy the unreconcileable ? Is it not simply the unreconciled ? And was the nature of Sophocles or of Shakespeare not ' conciliant ' ?

To pass now to a later strain of reflection : the subject had an especial fascination for Schopenhauer. His view is briefly expressed in the following paragraph (I quote from Mr. Haldane's English translation, vol. i. p. 327) :

' Tragedy is to be regarded, and is recognised, as the summit of poetical art, both on account of the greatness of its effect and the difficulty of its achievement. It is very significant for our whole system, and well worthy of observation, that the end of this highest poetical achievement is the representation of the terrible side of life. The unspeakable pain, the wail of humanity, the triumph of evil, the scornful mastery of chance, and the irretrievable fall of the just and innocent, is here presented to us ; and in

this lies a significant hint of the nature of the world
and of existence. It is the strife of will with itself,
which here, completely unfolded at the highest grade
of its objectivity, comes into fearful prominence. It
becomes visible in the suffering of men, which is
now introduced, partly through chance and error,
which appear as the rulers of the world, personified
as fate, on account of their insidiousness, which even
reaches the appearance of design ; partly it proceeds
from man himself, through the self-mortifying efforts
of a few, through the wickedness and perversity of
most. It is one and the same will that lives and
appears in them all, but these phenomena fight
against each other and destroy each other. In one
individual it appears powerfully, in another more
weakly ; in one more subject to reason, and softened
by the light of knowledge, in another less so ; till at
last in some single case, this knowledge, purified and
heightened by suffering itself, reaches the point at
which the phenomenon, the veil of Maya, no longer
deceives it. It sees through the form of phenomenon,
the *principium individuationis*. The egotism which
rests on this perishes with it, so that now the motives
which were so powerful before, have lost their might,
and instead of them the complete knowledge of the
nature of the world, which has a quieting effect on
the will, produces resignation, the surrender not
merely of life, but of the will to live . . . The true
sense of tragedy is the deeper insight, that it is not

his own individual sins that the hero atones for, but original sin, *i.e.* the crime of existence itself :

> " For the greatest crime of man
> Is that he was born,"

as Calderon exactly expresses it' (in 'Life is a Dream ').

In other words, the spectator of a perfect tragedy goes forth convinced that life is not worth living, and that the only reason against suicide is that, for one who is capable of such enjoyment, there is a temporary refuge in the charmed region of dramatic art. This point of view has been further elaborated by others whose aesthetic theory was more directly inspired by a passion for music, and especially by Friedrich Nietzsche, who in early days looked on the art of Richard Wagner as a new birth of Tragedy.

Nietzsche's view was altered in some respects when he reacted from the pessimistic theory of Schopenhauer, but his distinction between the Dionysiac and the Apolline element remains as a pregnant conception that is full of suggestiveness. It may have been derived by him from the Delphic legend according to which that centre of Greek religious life was occupied by the Apolline *cultus* after a contest in which the God of Light overcame the deity of wild inspiration. That story may have appeared to symbolise the growth of tragic art from crude beginnings towards a higher development.

Song, which, as Charles Darwin observed, has an important place in all animal life, is the natural accompaniment of each fresh access of vitality. There was a time when collective humanity simply revelled in the imagination of horrors. What thoughts were germinating in the mind of the tribe when at their Communion festival they tore in pieces the live victim that was the symbol and warrant of their union ? The act seems akin to madness ; yet in the impulse which led to it there was a religious fervour in which human joy and grief, hope and terror, resolution and despair, were blended in one overpowering emotion. This found vent not only in song, but in representative action. Imaginary scenes were invented to account for the wildness of the ceremonial, and fables thus originated lived on as legends into a more civilised period, when the community was bound within the limits of convention. Wise legislators found it expedient to give some indulgence to this survival from primitive times, and civilised man broke loose in fancy from the limits of the accustomed routine ; but the spirit of order was not thus really overborne. Apollo led Dionysus by a silken thread. The cultured rose blooms the more freely in that it is grafted on the wild native stock. For in the bosom of that untamed exuberance there stirred the pulses of a life more deeply interfused, anticipations of a wider, all-embracing law, that only waited for the hand of some poetic and religious genius, of a spirit 'touched to fine issues,' to draw them forth into forms of beauty and strength.

As has been already implied, there are undoubted links of affiliation between the two great periods, between the Greek and the English forms; but the relationship is slender and superficial.

(1) Such hybrid works as the 'Christus Patiens,' in which the dying embers of classical association were consecrated to Christian use, may have been present to the minds of some of those who originated the mystery play, or even to the author of such moralities as 'Everyman' or 'Lusty Juventus.' But, apart from tradition, such modes of incipient drama would probably have sprung up in connection with Christianity as with other religions. A writer in the *Athenæum* for January 16, 1904, in reviewing Captain Brinkley's work on Japan, makes the following statement: 'The drama in Japan was not one of the importations from China; it originated partly in the Nō, partly in the Kagura or sacred Mimes, representing originally the dance by which the gods induced the Sun-Goddess to issue from the cavern into which she had retired on receiving from her brother the strange insult of having a horse's hide flayed backwards thrown over her as she sat at her loom. Some learned folk see in this story a combination of myths founded upon eclipses and thunderstorms. The Nō were dialogues of a rather common

character interrupted by choral narrative songs made
up largely of tags from the collections of little verses
current in Japan from a very early time.   Of one of
these Nō—more correctly Nō nōutai, songs accompanying the Nō, which was a gesture dance—a full
translation will be found in the third volume.   The
subject is the story of Benkei and Yoshitsune, which
Captain Brinkley appears to accept as assured
history . . . The drama, however, though influenced
by Nō and Kagura, was not directly a product of
either, but the result of a master of the ceremonies
falling in love with a miko or Kagura vestal, in the
service of the Shogun Yoshiteru (middle of sixteenth
century).   Both were dismissed in consequence of
this breach of etiquette and took to performing
"rounds" or shibai—still the word for the theatre—
in the open air to gain a livelihood.'   Have we not
here an analogue at once of the waggon of Thespis
and of the transition from the sacred mystery or
morality to the Coventry plays, the wandering
pageant, and the interlude?

   (2) When from such beginnings there gradually
came into being a national theatre, such comedies as
' Gammer Gurton's Needle,' a crude form of tragedy,
and the chronicle play, the new and powerful breath
of the Renaissance was filling the air.   Here was
a second and a more substantial link between the
ancient and the modern.   But the classical drama
in England could not of itself produce a national

theatre. It was only when the culture of the
Renaissance descended amidst 'the rude jumble of
sport and earnest which the mob loved,' and con-
verted it into a source of imaginative and passionate
effects, that Marlowe stood forth as the herald of a
new era. And it was not, as we may well believe,
through any fresh study of the antique, that, in passing from Marlowe to Shakespeare, English drama
was humanised and harmonised, or that the raw
though stupendous force which created 'Tamburlaine'
gave place to the heart-affluence that inspired
'Romeo and Juliet,' 'Hamlet,' 'Macbeth,' 'Othello,'
and 'King Lear.'

It is therefore open to us, in attempting to draw
an historical parallel between the two epochs, to
consider them as independent 'births of time,' and
before entering more deeply upon the subject it
may be pointed out that the mythical and legendary
basis of Greek tragedy corresponds to the familiar
traditions of the English race. The Wars of the
Roses, for example, presented horrors comparable
with 'the Tale of Thebes or Pelops' line,' while the
Roman background of European civilisation had its
counterpart in the epic tale of Troy. And it may be
remarked incidentally that in both ages, the Attic
and the Elizabethan, the reading public was small
and the mass of the spectators were ready to accept
without critical inquiry a new version of a familiar
history.

It is a commonplace observation that the Elizabethan like the Attic development was consequent on a great national triumph, and if in the discomfiture of Philip II. as in that of Xerxes at Artemisium the elements played an important part, the feeling of exultation, tempered with thankfulness to a kind Providence, was not the less exalted in both. But deeper causes lay behind the national triumph. A Greek historian justly observes that Athenian heroism was the first-fruits of political liberty; and the outburst of fresh vitality, of which the Shakespearian drama was the flower and crown, was in like manner the offspring of a twofold emancipation of the human spirit, from scholasticism in the Renaissance, and in the Reformation from the power of Rome. The heightened consciousness of mankind in the Periclean age gave utterance for the first time to the conception of human nature as such, and in Elizabethan England the same conception, enriched by the gathered experience of two thousand years, found varied utterance; and nowhere more completely than in the drama.

In the following chapters there will be much to say of approximations in English tragic drama to the masterpieces of the Athenian stage; but it will not be forgotten that the approach is made from what in many ways may be regarded as an opposite pole: from the historic towards the universal; from incoherence to unity, or rather to harmony; from realism towards ideal truth; from a popular to a religious standpoint—in a word, from the Gothic towards the Greek; and it will be maintained that the secret of such an approach, so far as it is made, is not due to any immediate contact with the antique, but to dramatic genius instinctively realising essential principles of tragic art.

To speak more generally of the two periods in which tragic dramas of the highest order were composed, it may be said with truth of either of them that it was a time of great national triumphs, of world-wide interests, of great political crises, great attempts, great successes, great reverses; in which all the powers of humanity for good and evil were manifested with extraordinary energy. Experience does not lead us to suppose that tragedy is most enjoyed in times of exhaustion or depression. The reverse has really been the case. The mind in low states of vitality seeks for lighter modes of recreation and refreshment. It is then we hear it said, as is often repeated at the present day, 'Life is full of real unhappiness; why make us weep over imaginary woes?'

CHAPTER II

THE TRAGIC FABLE (ὁ μῦθος)

The fable not invented in the great periods—Reasons for this—
Principles of selection—Chief sources, ancient and modern—
Innovation with regard to subjects in the decline of the drama.

WILAMOWITZ-MÖLLENDORFF has thus described
Greek tragedy: 'An Attic tragedy is a portion of
heroic legend poetically elaborated in a lofty style
for production through a choir of Athenian citizens
and from two to three actors; intended for exhibition
within the sacred precinct of Dionysus as a part of
public divine service.' With this may be compared
the following sentence from 'The Idea of Tragedy'
by W. L. Courtney:

'For the ancient as for the modern artist the
problem was the same—so to carve out and fashion
a story from the great quarry of legendary tales,
that it should be a complete work in itself, with
a definite plot, definite characterisation, and definite
incidents leading up to the catastrophe.'

It was noted by Aristotle that the subjects
chosen for treatment by the tragic poets became
gradually restricted to critical events in the tradi-

tional histories of a few great houses. This remark
may suggest some observations as to the motives
which guide the tragic dramatist in the choice of
his fable.

The poet is of course free to select amongst
different versions of the same fable, and to modify
particular incidents ; *e.g.* in the common version of
the story of Lear, Cordelia survives and triumphs,
but Geoffrey of Monmouth says that she was hanged,
and this version is adopted with modification by
Shakespeare.

Taking now into one view the masterpieces
ancient and modern which we have selected for
consideration, we observe, *first*, that in every case
the story is one which had already taken hold of the
popular imagination. *Secondly*, in almost every
case it had already found embodiment in a literary
form, if it had not been previously thrown into
a dramatic shape. *Thirdly*, the course of events is
capable of such limits as to have a beginning, middle,
and end ; in other words there is a central crisis and
the possibility of a catastrophe which for the time is
final. The continuous treatment of several portions
of one history belongs either to the transitional
stage, as in the Aeschylean trilogies and the English
chronicle plays, or to an afterthought, as in the
' Oedipus Coloneus ' and the second part of ' Faust.'
Schiller's ' Wallenstein ' is in this respect an imitation
of the English historical play. It is observable that

in Shakespeare's ' Richard III.,' where for the first time history rises to the level of tragedy, the action is complete in itself, the antecedents being briefly summarised, and the conclusion, while looking forward to subsequent history, having the effect of finality and repose.[1]

Fourthly.—In each fable as regarded by the poet some aspect of human life considered as a whole is strikingly exemplified, and some master passion— revenge, love, jealousy, patriotism, political zeal— is developed to its highest power and tried to the uttermost.

Fifthly.—In most instances there is crime and retribution. Either the criminal is the chief agent and triumphs until suddenly cut off, as in ' The Jew of Malta,' ' Richard III.,' and ' Macbeth,' or the sufferer is the protagonist, and satisfaction lingers, as in ' Hamlet,' ' Othello,' and ' King Lear.'

Sixthly.—The fable is one which can be idealised so as to produce an impression of greatness both moral and material. Such ' naked tragedy' as the crime in ' Arden of Feversham ' cannot be made the vehicle of tragic drama in the highest sense.

Seventhly.—On the other hand the poet may be incidentally led by temporary associations to the choice of his theme. But critics and interpreters

---

[1] The drama of some peoples, the Chinese for example, seems to have been arrested at what I have called the transitional stage, of which perhaps the best example in English is Marlowe's *Tamburlaine*

have sometimes made too much of this, and have been diverted from the essential point. Thus it is possible that Aeschylus alludes to Aristides, to the Argive alliance, or to the limitation of the powers of the Areopagus. And even in Sophocles may be traced associations derived from the plague at Athens, from the expulsion of an accursed family, from the presence of the Spartan captives, or from conservative reaction. But the merit of his drama as a work of art is wholly independent of all this. Much vain ingenuity has been spent by Mr. Watkiss Lloyd and others in giving undue importance to such conjectures. And similarly G. Brandes, the Danish critic of Shakespeare, has laid excessive stress on the possible relation of several dramas to crises in the poet's life, suggesting, for example, that 'Hamlet' was written soon after his father's death, or that Volumnia reminded him of his mother. That a passage from a Scottish chronicle should be chosen for treatment after the accession of James I. was natural, and the allusion to Banquo's issue as ancestors of the Stuarts is obvious, yet how little this has to do with the tragic force of 'Macbeth'!

Eighthly.—In each case some great life is visited or threatened with downfall. The actuality of evil is contrasted with possibilities of good, and it depends partly upon the temperament of the poet and the spirit of his age in what proportion these two main elements are mixed.

No one of our three poets was ambitious of creating an original fable. After selecting for his purpose a cardinal event or incident from the body of tradition and fixing his thought upon the critical point, he sought to remould the tale and present it anew according to the bent and prompting of his original genius. In many cases the story had been already dramatised, but whether this were so or not there existed abundant material to work upon in epic narrative, in lyric song, in chronicle, ballad, or romance. Even Aeschylus, in choice of subject, more than once followed in the track of Phrynichus; but for the Tale of Thebes and Pelops' line, for the repulse of Ajax and the like he could draw from the successors of Homer in epic poetry, from Pindar, Stesichorus, and other lyric poets now lost to us, while for his theological and mythical subjects he could look back to the Hesiodic poems and probably to Orphic or Eleusinian hymns. Sophocles certainly in the selection of his fable was often content to follow his immediate predecessor's lead. In the 'Ajax,' the first 'Oedipus,' the 'Electra,' the 'Philoctetes,' he was on ground which the genius of Aeschylus had already consecrated, and in the 'Antigone' he developed a pregnant hint from the catastrophe of the 'Seven against Thebes.' In the 'Trachiniae,' however, he seems to have gone directly back to epic legend, and while the subject of the second 'Oedipus' still belongs to the Theban cycle, yet in adapting it to local associations, and to a motive of Athenian patriotism, he exercised to an unusual extent his own invention.

In Shakespearian tragedy the stories of 'Hamlet' and 'King Lear' had certainly been dramatised already, so possibly had those of 'Romeo and Juliet' and 'Othello'; for the rest Belleforest, Cinthio, the 'Palace of Pleasure,' Holinshed, and Plutarch provided a rich store, and how closely the given incidents are followed will appear when we come to speak of action and construction. The catastrophe in some cases is remodelled, single incidents are here and there invented as they follow naturally in the course of remoulding the events, different versions of the same story may be utilised to give dramatic relief,[1] but the creative imagination of the tragic poet shows itself not in this way but in the vividness with which the action is seized and presented as a whole, and the impressiveness with which it is evolved, in the light of profound thought and sympathetic emotion.

It is now well known that the legends inherited by various races in different ages from a pre-historic time, whether due to a common origin or not, are essentially similar, or at least analogous; and those in particular which awaken pity and fear are limited in their range and turn upon a few chief motives.

---

[1] As in the *Ajax*, *Macbeth*, and *King Lear*, where, as above stated, the death of Cordelia is adapted from Geoffrey of Monmouth.

The awe-striking vicissitudes of great fortunes, the judgment following on defiance of religious sanctions, especially those which surround the family or the race —ill-weaved ambition over-leaping itself, the misuse of power, jealousy prevailing against love, the crimes of one generation leaving a burden of vengeance to the next, the wrath aroused by filial ingratitude drawing down curses terribly fulfilled—these and such-like strands appear and reappear in the varied web of tradition. The ancient *répertoire* is further restricted by the identity of motive in different legends; the story of Alcmaeon is that of Orestes over again. Thus there is a real analogy inherent in the fable between Oedipus the King and the tyranny of Macbeth, between Orestes and Hamlet, between the sons of Oedipus and the daughters of King Lear. Some understanding of this fact is necessary as a preliminary consideration, whether the intention is to compare or to contrast the creations of ancient and modern drama. The germs are analogous, however disparate may be the resulting forms.

Take for example the frequently observed analogy between the position of Hamlet and that of Orestes. An ambitious relative has seduced the Queen, has compassed the death of the King, and usurped the throne. The son and heir of the slain monarch is charged with the duty of revenge. These are the elements of the tale in both cases; how differently they are handled by Aeschylus, Sophocles, and

Shakespeare, how far this has arisen from differences in the spirit of the age or of individual genius, and how far these varieties of dramatic treatment are subordinate to analogous tendencies of tragic art, is the matter to be studied. In the story of Oedipus the unnatural conduct of his sons is contrasted with the true affection of his daughters; in the story of Lear the unnatural daughters are contrasted with Cordelia; but the leading motive in either tale is strikingly similar.

It is an instructive fact that in the case of either drama novelties with regard to subject were only introduced when the great period was already passing. Fletcher and Massinger were ambitious of inventing their fables, and although the stock instance of Agathon's 'Flower' is perhaps due to an erroneous reading in the 'Poetics,' it is indubitable that Euripides in his later vein, while formally remaining within the legendary cycle, indulged his inventiveness with great boldness in remodelling tradition. Thus one source of dramatic illusion was at once abandoned. For, as Aristotle puts it, what is believed to have really happened, however strange, is accepted as possible. But as time went on a sophisticated audience cared less to be impressed with the reality of what they saw than to be stimulated by novelties of situation and character. Hence Jacobean dramatists ransacked the romantic and dramatic literature of Italy and Spain for striking effects, which they combined through the original exercise of their invention, with the object of holding the theatre in suspense, and surprising the audience with some unlooked-for *dénouement*. But, as Mr. Courthope has said, 'How can the reader' (or spectator) 'feel fear, pity, joy, or grief in situations which are obviously artificial and in which the dramatists themselves have not taken the trouble to observe the laws of external probability necessary to produce illusion?'

Massinger's 'Virgin Martyr' is clearly indebted to the 'El Magico Prodigioso' of Calderon. The machinery is similar and the demon's flight from the Christian symbol is alike in both. But the effect of what might else have been a beautiful production is marred by the English demand for brutal business on the stage and by the lubricity of the Jacobean epoch.

CHAPTER III

TRAGIC ACTION (τὸ δρᾶμα)

A great crisis in a great life—Greatness, both outward and inward—
Fate and free will in ancient and modern tragedy—The English
taste for action on the stage—How far condescended to by Shakespeare—The influence of circumstance—The action developed
from the fable—Universality of motive—Continuity—Proportion
between horror and pity.

THE action is the fable dramatised. Every tragic
action consists of a great crisis in some great life,
not merely narrated but presented in act, through
language, in such a way as to move the hearts of
those who see and hear. This description is equally
true of the Athenian and the Shakespearian drama.
The greatness is at once outward and inward. The
crisis is the meeting point of a great personality
with great surroundings. As Mr. W. L. Courtney
puts it, 'tragedy is always a clash of two powers—
necessity without, freedom within; outside, a great,
rigid, arbitrary law of fate; inside, the undefeated individual will, which can win its spiritual triumph even
when all its material surroundings and environment
have crumbled into hopeless ruin. . . . . Necessity
without, liberty within—that is the great theme

which, however disguised, runs through every tragedy that has been written in the world.' [1]

But it is commonly assumed that whereas in Aeschylus and Sophocles the necessity is wholly outward, in Shakespeare it is the direct outcome of personality; that while the theme of ancient drama is, as Wordsworth says:

> ' Poor humanity's afflicted will
> Struggling in vain with ruthless destiny,'

in Shakespeare the tragic hero is encountered by the consequences of his own errors; so that here, far more than in the Greek masterpieces, we see exemplified the truth of the Greek proverb ' Character is destiny'; 'no fate broods over the actions of men, and the history of families; the only fatality is the fatality of character' (Dowden).

This is only partly true. All ancient art and thought is in form more objective, while an ever-growing subjectivity is the note of the modern mind; and the ancient fables mostly turned on some pre-determined fatality. But in his moulding of the fable the Attic poet was guided by his own profound conception of human nature as he saw it in its freest working. The idea of fate is thus, as it were, expanded into an outer framework for the picture of life, except in so far as it remains to symbolise those inscrutable causes beyond human control, whose working is likewise present to the

[1] On Free Will and Fortune see Machiavelli's *Prince*, c. 25.

mind of Shakespeare. Xerxes, Agamemnon, Clytemnestra, Ajax, Creon, are no less the victims of
their own passionate errors than Macbeth or Lear;
and the fate of Hamlet almost equally with that
of Oedipus is due to antecedent and surrounding
circumstances with which neither he nor any man
could have power to cope; although here also
malign fortune is assisted by 'the o'ergrowth of
some complexion, Oft breaking down the pales and
forts of reason.' Of this more will be said hereafter. Meanwhile, a neglected passage from one
of Wordsworth's essays (1815) is worth recalling.
'It is a current opinion that Shakespeare is justly
praised when he is pronounced to be a " wild, irregular
genius in whom great faults are compensated for by
great beauties." How long may it be before this
misconception passes away, and it becomes uni-
versally acknowledged that the judgment of Shakespeare, in the selection of his materials, and in the
manner in which he has made them, heterogeneous
as they often are, constitute a unity of their own,
and contribute all to one great end, is not less
admirable than his imagination, his invention, and
his intuitive knowledge of human nature?'

In one sense action had a more prominent place
in the Elizabethan than in the modern drama. The
English audience, then and always, has been greedy
of witnessing actual business on the stage. They
loved to see the Oriental kings, those 'jades of Asia,'

cruelly harnessed to the car of Tamburlaine; the putting out of Gloster's eyes, the murder of Banquo, would, in an Athenian drama, have been reported and not seen—not merely to avoid what is repulsive (τὸ μιαρόν), but to preserve proportion. The profoundly moving events which form the action of the first 'Oedipus' are presented almost entirely through dialogue. But in this point also Shakespeare's method at its best approximates to the antique. Suppose, for example, in the great scenes of 'Macbeth,' Act I. Scenes v. and vi., Act II. Scenes i. and ii., the poet had gone the whole way to meet the demand in question. The spectator would then have been introduced to the chamber where Duncan lay calmly asleep, and would have heard the stertorous snoring of the grooms. The prayer and the 'Amen' of Donalbain and his bedfellow would likewise have been audible. Macbeth would have been seen not following an air-drawn dagger, but with a real dirk in hand, while Lady Macbeth just peeped through the half-opened door, whispering incitements to her husband as he hesitated to strike; until the blow was given and the deed was done. To the vulgar apprehension this tableau might have given an impression of horror more distinct than it receives from the soliloquies and the dialogue, but there can be no question which method answers most completely to the ideal of tragic *action*.

The action in all the plays under consideration has

external as well as internal elements of greatness. The fatal jealousy of Othello, that so racks and tortures our sympathies, owes much of its effect to the downfall of the great soldier whose career had been the salvation of the Venetian empire. Macbeth was first the deliverer, and then the ruin of a kingdom. The fate of Hamlet, indeed, is the more pitiful because of the meanness and narrowness of the actual Danish court; but his father had been a great conqueror, and by the admission of Fortinbras he himself had he been ' put on ' would have achieved nobly. It is needless to enforce the same consideration with regard to Attic tragedy, which, whether the scene is laid at Thebes or in Argos or elsewhere, turns on the fortunes of great houses and the destinies of States which relatively are represented as great. For to the Athenian spectator that ' bright Aegean nook ' was all the world.

As the value of the individual has gradually been more appreciated in the evolution of the race, there has arisen in some minds the notion of a ' soul's tragedy ' which might be realised independently of external antecedents and surrounding circumstances. But such an ideal has never yet been made effective in dramatic presentation before a popular audience, or taken its place as a factor in national drama.

The main situation is always inherent in the fable, and not impressed upon it from without. This

is well expressed by G. H. Lewes in his strictures on
Calderon :

'When people talk of Calderon as an artist, and
even Goethe told Eckermann that he thought Calderon infinitely great in whatever was technical and
theatrical, they think only of the powerful situations
he invents, but forget the means by which these are
brought about. Yet precisely therein lies the artist's
difficulty. It is not, I imagine, difficult to suggest
powerful dramatic situations, but to make them
naturally evolve from the characters and circumstances of the play, to make them consistent with
human motives, this is the problem for the artist,
and only he deserves the name who can satisfactorily
solve that problem. Sophocles does this, Shakespeare
does it, Molière does it, Racine does it ; in Calderon
it is a rarity. Art consists in evolving from within
organically, not in mechanical juxtaposition of
materials.' A very similar precept was enjoined
upon the Indian dramatic poet.[1]

Every masterpiece of tragic drama has a universal
aspect and intention. The choice of the fable may
have been partly due to temporary associations, but
the action has a world-wide significance. The 'Ajax'
of Sophocles appealed to an Athenian audience
through their pride in the memories of Salamis and
their adoption of the son of Telamon as a national
hero. But the drama owes its unfading interest to

[1] See Monier-Williams' *Sakuntala*.

the poet's profound realisation of the effect of
wounded honour on the mind of a soldier. All that
is of temporary or local interest is subordinated to
this profoundly human motive—not a mere conventional point of honour as in the Spanish drama,
or in the 'Cid' of Corneille, where the pathos appeals
only to a limited class, but an emotion to which all
hearts in every age cannot but respond.

The action is one and continuous. It is needless
to dwell upon the once famous unities. Even on
the Attic stage there are exceptions to Aristotle's
requirement of a limit of twenty-four hours. Both
in the 'Agamemnon' and 'Antigone' time is clearly
foreshortened, not to mention the long interval
between the opening and the main action of the
'Eumenides'; and although the presence of the
Chorus ordinarily binds the imagination of the spectator to a single spot (the 'scene individable'), yet
there are notable exceptions, where the orchestra is
left vacant for a time to allow for a change of scene,
and it is possible that such a change may have
occurred between the prologue and the entrance of
the Chorus in the 'Oedipus Coloneus.'

Shakespeare of course claims a much larger
liberty with regard to both place and time, but the
action is notwithstanding one. In 'King Lear' indeed there is a concurrent action, or underplot, but
this is studiously subordinated to the central interest,

with which it is so interwoven as not only har-
moniously to set it off, but to be an integral portion
of the whole. In some cases both ancient and
modern there is observable a certain polarity of
interest, two persons being involved in the main
action, which is notwithstanding one. This happens
in the case of Oedipus and Jocasta, Antigone and
Creon, Deianira and Heracles, Antony and Cleopatra,
Lear and Cordelia ; but the unity of interest and of
impression is not thus destroyed.

Another common feature of these great works is
continuity. The action is developed not through
ingenious invention, but through the natural effect
of incident and situation in bringing about the
central movement. It may be well to quote the
example of a famous play which fails in this respect.
In Ford's ' Broken Heart ' there is a succession of
crises rising in intensity until the famous scene in
which the news of her lover's death is whispered to
Calantha at the festival. But the centre of gravity,
so to speak, is changed again and again, and the
spectator's sympathies are consequently distracted.
We are led to believe at the outset that the main
interest is to centre in Orgilus and Penthea, but by
a sudden turn in the catastrophe our sympathies are
absorbed in Calantha. For poignancy of effect this
scene can hardly be excelled, but the unity of action
is destroyed. The surprise would have pleased a
French dramatist, and it was by similar means that

Euripides earned the epithet of 'most tragic'; but the method is alien from the moderation of Sophocles or of Shakespeare. The revenge of Orgilus, carried out in the cruellest way after his enemy's heart had been softened towards him, is shocking to the moral sense. It creates a painful surprise like that in the 'Orestes' of Euripides, when it is suddenly proposed to assassinate Helen. Penthea's moral martyrdom is pathetic enough, but our sorrow for her is tempered with amusement at the comic antics of her husband, which strike a false note. He should have been odious but not laughably so. Moreover the dazzling effect of the final scene inevitably obliterates all the preceding impressions, and although the character of Penthea is well drawn it is difficult to acquit her of hypocrisy either in her repulse of Orgilus or her still more virtuous submissiveness to Bassanes. Both turn more on the point of honour than on any higher principle. Shakespeare's plan is to interest us more and more from the beginning in the chief person, and in the main situation; then, by successive complications of the action to raise sympathetic emotion to a height of suspense, until the crisis is past; after this, while the altered situation no longer excites the same interest of uncertainty, it is held before the mind in such a way as to deepen the awe and pity which have been called forth, until the action proceeds to the unavoidable catastrophe. Such unity of impression is absent from 'The Broken Heart.'

Another drawback no less fatal is where the central personality is repulsive or uninteresting. In Otway's ' Venice Preserved,' the action hinges on the person of Jaffier, who is pulled in two directions alternately by love and friendship. He proves himself unworthy alike of Belvidera his mistress and Pierre his friend. This destroys the tragic interest and results in what Matthew Arnold would have called ' a broken-backed sort of thing.'

In the great dramas the action is carried forward with every scene so that a climax of emotional interest is steadily maintained up to the turning-point. This is hardly the case in Dryden's ' All for Love,' where, in spite of his effort after unity, the dialogue between Antony and Ventidius in the first act is more interesting than anything which follows —as Dryden himself confessed.

Once more, in a great tragic action there is always a certain balance or proportion between horror and pity. It may well be doubted for example whether in Webster's ' Duchess of Malfi ' our compassion for the victim with whose blameless passion we have sympathised is not too violently overborne by the revulsion of feeling akin to incredulity which is produced by the deliberate accumulation of agonies in the catastrophe.

As Shakespeare has not complicated tragedy with an underplot except in the case of ' King Lear,' it is unnecessary to contrast his supremely harmonious treatment of the twofold action with the ' tragi-comedies ' of his contemporaries and successors. It is enough to observe that when the subordinate tragedy is closed by the death of Edmund, who had been its mainspring, and on whom also so much of the principal action had depended, Albany can say with the entire concurrence of the bystanders and of the audience, ' That's but a trifle here.'

CHAPTER IV

TRAGIC PERSONS—CHARACTERISATION (τὰ ἤθη).

Characterisation in Shakespeare and Sophocles—Types and indi-
    viduals—The Achilles of Homer—' The solidity of the antique '
    —Contrasted persons—The reaction of situation on character—
    Supremacy of Shakespeare.

IN Attic tragedy taken as a whole the persons are
subordinated to the action and to the main situation.
In Shakespeare the abounding wealth of his
characterisation is apt to predominate over his
management of the fable. But in both there is
observable a gradual development towards a perfect
form in which the two factors interpenetrate and are
inextricably fused in one. In the earlier dramas of
Aeschylus the chief persons are sketched out by
means of a few masterly strokes. First lyrical
effusion, then epic narration fill up the greater part
of the scheme. But in the later scenes of the
' Agamemnon ' the poet attains a height of dramatic
portraiture which has hardly been surpassed, and in
the ' Antigone ' and ' Ajax ' of Sophocles the heroic
persons already stand forth with full distinctness
and are contrasted with subordinate agents. In

Shakespeare's 'Richard III.' the historic background is made the occasion for an elaborate and impressive presentation of the royal villain, and in the person of Margaret, as a human Nemesis, the characterisation approaches the solidity of the antique. At the same time the action is swift, uninterrupted, and complete. But it is in the latest tragedies that the interplay of character and situation and the reaction of the persons on one another are both wrought out with profound psychological subtilty and so conducted as to insure the impressiveness of the action as a whole.

It is often said that the ancient drama presented types rather than individuals. That in this, as in other respects, simplicity is the note of the antique, is perfectly true. But the outlines are so firm and strong, and the forms are modelled out of such a depth of human experience, that our belief in the reality of Clytemnestra, Oedipus, Ajax, Antigone, Philoctetes, Phaedra, and Medea, as real individuals, is almost as ineffaceable as our recognition of Hamlet, Lady Macbeth, Othello, Lear, and Imogen ; and Shakespeare's persons also when critically considered may likewise be regarded as typical.

Another current notion is that fate in the ancient drama is all in all, while for Shakespeare character takes the place of fate in determining the catastrophe. That, as already indicated, is not altogether true. For the Attic poet a blind destiny,

or a Providence more or less malignant, formed part
of the traditional data on which he worked. For
Shakespeare, in like manner, the course of events
was prescribed by the fable. But in both cases the
work of creative imagination gave a human and
probable interpretation to the crude material. No
dramas are more evidently tragedies of doom than
the first ' Oedipus ' and the ' Trachiniae.' Yet how
clearly the effect of character on the event is trace-
able in both. |The impetuosity of the beneficent
tyrant, rushing to conclusions in reliance on his gift
of insight that is baffled by the hidden powers ;
the pathetic light which is thrown by his essential
innocence and public spirit upon the horror of
his discovery| the loving and constant heart of
Deianira, cajoled like Imogen's by false intelligence
referring to her lord and guilefully entrapping her
through the very strength of her affection—these
can hardly be said in truth of delineation to fall
short of their Shakespearian counterparts ; and,
on the other hand, in Shakespeare, the effect of
accident, or in other words of special Providence, is
not less marked than in Sophocles, and is likewise
accounted for by the inscrutable working of a divine
power.

Plato, generalising in his synoptic way, speaks of
Homer as the prince of tragedy ; and certainly the
Achilles of the ' Iliad ' is the ideal of what a tragic

hero should be ; composed of passion (inordinate
pride, tender love, devoted friendship), he is the
central figure of the greatest historic epoch of past
times, and his emotion, that of a nature essentially
noble, is the pivot of the action ending in his death.
Wounded in his love and in his sense of personal
dignity, and sternly withdrawing from the contest
until moved by the entreaty of his friend—that
friend's loss, overwhelming other emotions, at last
brings him into the field and prompts him to the
fatal encounter. Thus the crisis of the action and
the change of fortune are spontaneously evolved from
the personal characteristics which bring about the
catastrophe. Here then is the ' one tragic subject '
which, as Aristotle perceived, is supplied by the elder
epic.

The limitations of the Attic drama afforded less
scope for the production of so grand a *rôle*. Dealing
with one main situation, and with one critical
moment of an individual destiny, it could not give such
ample delineation to the principal figure. Eteocles,
the first hero who is elaborately portrayed by Aeschylus, impresses the spectator by the intensity of
his patriotic fervour, and his unflinching resolution
in the presence of imminent doom. But the climax
is well sustained, for, on the approach of his rebellious
brother, his passion becomes uncontrollable, defying
the destiny which he knows to be in store for himself, and realising for the spectator all the horror of

the paternal curse. The downfall of Macbeth when
he tries the last combat with the Avenger 'of no
woman born' is less pathetically impressive than
the death of the defender of Thebes. And, notwithstanding their simplicity, it is not altogether true
that tragic persons in Aeschylus and Sophocles are
unchanging or unaffected by circumstances. Clytemnestra would not be a tragic heroine if the bare
determination for vengeance were not mingled, on
the one hand with maternal affection, and on the
other with a real attachment to her unworthy
paramour. Nor should the presence in her of 'compunctious visitings' and a natural horror of blood-
guiltiness be altogether ignored. This appears in
the conclusion of the 'Agamemnon,' as well as in
the confused cry of pain which escapes from her
at the false news of Orestes' death, and the genuine
pathos of her appeal for mercy which accentuates
the dreadfulness of the matricide in the 'Choephori.'
Antigone's resolution never wavers; yet, rooted as
it is in love, it suffers from the natural reaction of
other feelings proper to her age, and in her last
scene she is well aware of all that she has sacrificed.
The resolve of Ajax is equally unwavering; but his
first passionate expression of it is succeeded by the
calm deliberation of the dissembling speech, which
is again contrasted with his last utterance, when he
pours forth all his resentment and all his affection
in one comprehensive cry. It is needless to dwell

on the changes in Deianira's mood, or on the conflict in the soul of Neoptolemus; and whereas in the Creon of the 'Antigone' or in Philoctetes the fixed idea suddenly gives way, this may be compared with the change in Shakespeare's Coriolanus, where a stubborn unyielding attitude is finally overborne. Electra alone answers fully to the conception of what is called the 'solidity of the antique'; her vindictiveness is equalled throughout by her filial affection which is its foundation, and by the yearning towards her brother.

The contrast and co-ordination of personalities, so essential to dramatic effect, was difficult so long as only two actors could be presented together in one scene. The addition of the third actor is ascribed to Sophocles, and although Aeschylus availed himself of the innovation, he did so sparingly, even in the Orestean trilogy. Yet the contrasted figures of Clytemnestra and Cassandra, the revengeful queen and the captive prophetess, her rival victim, though they are seen together only for a moment, give occasion for the most tragic of all extant scenes, concentrating the emotions which meet in the culminating point of the 'Agamemnon.' The Sophoclean contrasts between Antigone and Ismene, Electra and Chrysothemis, Philoctetes and Neoptolemus, are too familiar to be described at length. It is enough to remark that the wonderful skill with which Shakespeare groups the principal and subordinate persons of his drama was anticipated upon the Attic stage ; and in particular that the introduction side by side with the tragic hero of ' the man who is not passion's slave,' of Horatio with Hamlet, of Banquo with Macbeth, of Kent with Lear, is analogous to the employment by Sophocles of such persons as Creon in the first ' Oedipus,' Odysseus in the ' Ajax,' and Theseus in the ' Oedipus Coloneus.'

Dramatic criticism has too often proceeded on the assumption that the function of the dramatist is merely the presentation or creation of character, or the psychological delineation of emotions. Tragic drama consists not merely in character study, nor in the vivid interplay of personalities, but in the action of character on situation and of situation upon character. The action rightly conceived is the resultant of these cardinal forces. The environment of circumstance is not merely harmonised with the chief person or with his ruling passion, but it is imagined as evolving both. ' Character is destiny ' ; yes, but not in the sense that certain elements of personality have predestined the chief agent to a certain doom. The pity of it combined with awe and horror turns upon our conviction that in other circumstances the possibilities of evil which for the time have triumphed might have been overruled by still greater possibilities of good. Place Hamlet somewhere else than in the Danish court, let him succeed to the peaceful possession of a throne, give him worthy objects for his love and reverence, and adequate leverage for beneficent activity, and the splendid powers of action which come out spasmodically in foiling the plot against his life, in his manipulation of the players to his purpose of discovery, and his final vindication of the right, would have assured to him a magnificent career; his princely courtesy, his genial good-fellowship, the heartiness of his attachment, would have secured to him the happiness, the popularity, and the outward success which his inherent nobleness deserved. The strain of passionateness which being suppressed and thwarted breaks out so as to ruin his main design would have been the spring of great achievements, the inspiration of high and daring deeds. His deep thoughts, his penetrating insight, his far-reaching speculative vein, which, as it is, are all turned inwards and 'lose the name of action,' might then have found free range and scope so as to be full of blessing. When this is ignored, he is regarded as a born dreamer, for whom, as for Coleridge, the very name of duty paralyses will. Such a personality would be less than tragic.

Similarly when Macbeth is looked upon as a mere scoundrel in grain, whose imagination of a virtuous life only gives zest to his career of crime, he ceases to be a tragic hero, and the grandest *rôle* in Shakespeare is degraded into a mere character part.

It is because the double nature in him reveals better possibilities, which but for fatal incitements and overmastering opportunity might have assured an honourable career, that we retain enough of sympathetic feeling for him to receive a tragic impression from the drama.

In richness and depth of characterisation, Shakespeare undoubtedly stands alone.[1] All for which I contend in this chapter is that in the development of Attic tragedy from the 'Persae' of Aeschylus to the 'Philoctetes' of Sophocles there is a steady growth in this respect towards a kindred treatment of human nature. The subtle gradations through which Neoptolemus is drawn from his purpose to entangle Philoctetes by deceit, the struggle of a new-found friendship with a cherished ambition, until at length his native honour and truth complete the sacrifice of self, is hardly less subtle in its complexity than the ruin of Othello.

[1] 'The characters in every drama must indeed be grouped; but in the groups of other poets the parts which are not seen do not in fact exist. But there is a certain roundness and integrity in the forms of *Shakespeare*, which give them an independence as well as a relation, insomuch that we often meet with passages which, though perfectly felt, cannot be sufficiently explained in words without unfolding the whole character of the speaker. . . . It is true that the point of action or sentiment, which we are most concerned in, is always held out for our special notice. But who does not perceive that there is peculiarity about it, which conveys a relish of the whole? And very frequently, when no particular point presses, he boldly makes a character act and speak from those parts of the composition which are *inferred* only, and not distinctly shown. This produces a wonderful effect: it seems to carry us beyond the

In the evolution of character through situation, Shakespeare's tragic art is unrivalled and supreme. But just as his persons may be contrasted in this respect with those of Thomas Heywood, of Beaumont and Fletcher, or of Massinger, whose heroes and heroines pass from mood to mood without assignable motive, so the changing attitude of persons in the Sophoclean drama may be contrasted with corresponding transitions in Euripides. The breakdown of Creon's stubborn resolution is in true accordance with his character, which alternates between scepticism and superstition, and with his fanatical anxiety for the welfare of the State. The *idée fixe* in the mind of Philoctetes is likewise suddenly overcome; but to effect this the intervention of his deified elder comrade, long lost and deeply revered, was indispensable. The more gradual changes in Antigone, Ajax, Oedipus, Deianira are delineated with admirable adherence to

poet to nature itself, and gives an integrity and truth to facts and character, which they could not otherwise obtain. And this is in reality that art in *Shakespeare*, which, being withdrawn from our notice, we more emphatically call *nature*. A felt propriety and truth from causes unseen, I take to be the highest point of Poetic Composition. If the characters of *Shakespeare* are thus whole, and as it were original, while those of almost all other writers are mere imitation, it may be fit to consider them rather as Historic than as Dramatic beings; and, when occasion requires, to account for their conduct from the *whole* of character, from general principles, from latent motives, and from policies not avowed.'—Maurice Morgann, *An Essay on the Dramatic Character of Sir John Falstaff*. 1777.

psychological truth. Can this be said for example
of the repentance of Hermione in the 'Andromache'
of Euripides ? Does it not lie open to the objection
of Aristotle, who in speaking of the altered mood
of Iphigenia says, 'she is no longer the same
person' ?

CHAPTER V

TRAGIC IDEAS (διάνοια)

Great tragedy not pessimistic—The tragic situation exceptional—
Universality—Tragic ideas in Aeschylus, Sophocles, and Shake
speare—Machiavellianism renounced by Shakespeare—Humanity
—Religion—The Supernatural—Poetical justice not required—
General maxims borrowed or original.

'Men are divided in their opinions whether our pleasures over-
balance our pains; and whether it be, or be not, eligible to live in
this world.'—Bishop Butler.

It is true of every great tragic poet that he 'saw
life steadily, and saw it whole'; but he saw it in the
light of his own genius and of the spirit of his age.
It was an age—not in which philosophy had formulated and systematised abstract categories of thought
and feeling—but one in which the best minds,
through keen sympathetic observation added to
vivid experience, had obtained a supreme power
of insight into the ruling motives, the dominant
passions, the errors and achievements, the success
and failure of mankind. It belongs to the conception of tragic drama that it turns upon some great
struggle between good and evil, between right and
wrong. Even if Hegel's formula were accepted, that
the opposition is of right to right, the fact of such

opposition is of itself an evil, a hindrance to the predominance of good.   In the earlier or crude form of the art in Greece the opposition lay between human endeavour and destiny, or divine malignity. In the mediaeval mystery, or morality play, there was a corresponding antithesis between the worldly life of pleasure and ambition and the spiritual law of renunciation embodied in the authority of the Church.   In so far the beginnings of the art would seem to justify the imputation of pessimism.   But it is not so with any one of the three great poets whom we are considering.   They are certainly engaged in sounding the depths of human evil ; but in doing so they exhibit in the clearest light the power and reality of the good.

It is too often assumed that tragedy aims at representing life in its normal aspect ; but the very poignancy of its effect is owing to the fact that the tragic fable is regarded as exceptional—that the downfall, where it is accomplished, was avoidable, had either the person or the circumstances been other than they were.   The necessity against which the will is striving is not an absolute necessity. The human being, after all, is gifted with a limited freedom, else why should the spectator be held in anxious suspense until the change of fortune has taken place, or why, if the sequel were inevitable, should it move him so profoundly?

Each poet, as has been said, shares the spirit of

his age, but the spirit of the age of Pericles and of that
of Elizabeth was also a spirit which had a voice for
all time. The drama of Calderon, though his tragic
genius is indisputable, was limited by the predominance of two motives from which Aeschylus,
Sophocles, and Shakespeare are alike free—the
Spanish point of honour, belonging to a class and
not to the nation at large, and the doctrines of the
Counter-Reformation reviving the mediaeval notion
of the nothingness of earthly things. At single
points even Calderon breaks loose from each of
these, as when the Mayor of Zalamea opposes his
right of manhood and paternity to military etiquette,
and where, in ' El Magico Prodigioso,' to our surprise,
the necessity of mediators between the Divine and
the Human is called in question.

Here for a moment the Spanish poet rises into
the sphere of tragic drama at its best.

Universality, then, is the test of tragic feeling ;
the emotion is interpenetrated with thought, the
sympathy is informed with insight, and the presentation at once of character and situation appeals
not merely to some section of humanity, but to man
as man. When we consider all that is involved in
this, it is evident that the poet has far outlived the
egoistic absorption in mere personal experience. If
even lyric poetry comes of ' emotion recollected in
tranquillity,' how much more must this be true of
one who seeks to produce a great impression through

the presentation of some cardinal aspect of human
life regarded as a whole ? That cannot fail to be
the supreme result of ' disinterested objectivity.'
The serious dramatist must have attained a height
from which, in a different way from the philosopher,
he has become the ' spectator of all time, and of all
existence.' Arriving at a moment when human life
both personal and national has been stirred by great
events into exceptional passionate activity, he takes
up the art at the stage at which he finds it, and the
fable as he receives it from his predecessors, perhaps
in some crude form in which it is dominated by an
unenlightened pessimism ; such as was in Ionia the
superstition of divine malignity, or, as in the sixteenth
century, the ignorant fear of wicked powers inspired
by so-called Machiavellianism ; and out of such
unformed rudiments he creates a new birth of time,
which he transfuses not with a doctrine of despair,
but with that wiser optimism which fearlessly confronts the utmost possibilities of evil in the faith
that there exist eternally still greater possibilities of
good.

All our three poets, if looked at in this general
way, are found to be partakers of one spirit, yet with
diversity of operations. Aeschylus, uplifted on the
wave of Hellenic progress, looked back upon the
confusions of an earlier world, and saw in them a
struggle towards the light of Athenian equity. The
lawless and uncertain thoughts of a past age were

moralised by the Eleusinian prophet. In the history of his own people from Miltiades to Aristides, in which he personally had taken an active share, he saw the rising of a spirit that was not to be overcome of evil, but, as he believed, was destined to overcome the evil with good. He exulted in a redemption of humanity which he saw to be at hand, and which among his own countrymen he believed to have begun. For Sophocles that mirage had partly been dispelled. He looked with steady, serene, and solemn gaze upon the actual world, and saw there good and evil, balanced and commingled. But over all he saw the light of an ideal—supreme, unchanging, ultimate—a law of piety, faithfulness, and purity, whose embodiment in human life is independent of the changes and chances of caprice or fortune; 'builded far from accident,' the outcome of 'that primal sympathy which, having been, must ever be.' He availed himself of the tragic fables at his command to help men to realise what is most worth living for, and draw their minds away from narrow cares and petty troubles to the practical contemplation of universal good and evil.

The two great tragic poets of Athens both looked at the facts of life through the medium of a religious feeling. Aeschylus, at once poet and prophet, had the vision of a righteousness exceeding that of priest and lawgiver, which he imagined as being realised through the divinely ordered course of human events.

Sophocles, with less immediate hope for the future of humanity, was not less deeply convinced of the supremacy of eternal principles, whose sanction was the inevitable consequence of all transgression, whether conscious or unconscious. The thought of Aeschylus was in one sense more transcendental, instinct with bold speculations concerning the divine attributes; but in another way he was more plunged in the concrete; even his Prometheus never loses sight of human misery and its relief. His contemplation, however, is extended to the race, while that of Sophocles centres more in an individual destiny. The poetry of Aeschylus is at once supra-mundane and intensely human; like Strife in Homer:—'Her head is in the firmament, her feet are on the ground.' Both dramas are dominated by a moral ideal, but the relation of the ideal to the actual is diversely conceived.

Although philosophy and poetry move on different planes, an illustration may sometimes be instructively drawn from one to the other. Aeschylus and Sophocles differed in their modes of contemplating life much as Heraclitus and Parmenides differed in their theories of universal being. Human history for Aeschylus was a process of evolution from moral chaos to moral cosmos, worked out through the war of contraries and ever tending towards a concrete harmony; this may be compared with Heraclitus' 'upward way.' The downward way of dissolution is also held before the mind as a perpetual danger, but such fear is overborne by the presiding hope.

For Sophocles, behind and above the sadness which he portrays—at once comprehending and transcending it—stands the vision of the moral law which is the same from everlasting. In this conception both horror and pathos are ultimately resolved, but they are not the less keenly felt, although poet and spectator alike know that there is a fixed centre amidst the moving scene. Hence results what has been called the 'irony of Sophocles,' which is nothing else than the contrast between fleeting appearances and abiding realities, which pervades the whole dramatic action and is subtly indicated by many turns of language.

The law of righteousness for both Greek poets had its centre in the sacredness of the family as the only secure foundation for the State. The reverence for the marriage bond, for the relation of child to parent, and parent to child; the dues of natural affection between sisters and brothers; the sanctity of the domestic hearth, are conceptions which appear and re-appear as essential motives. The awe and dread which brood over the Aeschylean scene involve no touch of asceticism. Aphrodite has her rights no less than Artemis, as the daughters of Danaus and of Oceanus alike acknowledge.

Among the blessings promised by the Eumenides

is the perfect union of hearts between man and maid. The poet's hatred of the denaturalised woman, the milk of whose affections some great outrage has turned to gall, is in proportion to the tenderness with which he regards the innocent inexperienced maiden and such a victim as Cassandra.

The idea of equity or of divine righteousness is closely associated with that of mercy to the unfortunate. To revere the suppliant is of course a leading rule in all Greek drama. Compassion for the captive is another aspect of the same feeling. The chorus of the Theban women in the 'Septem,' the appeal of Tecmessa in the 'Ajax,' are obvious instances of this, and more striking than either is the speech of Deianira in the 'Trachiniae,' expressing her warm feeling towards Iole, before she knows the truth. Whether the poet intended it or not, and I am inclined to think he did mean it so, some noble Athenian matron who had seen the men from Pylos may have had her maternal heart called forth into human sympathy by those touching words.

The conditions of the art demanded that these ideas of justice and mercy, of the family, of native country, of friendship and humanity, should be given through the troubled medium of passionate emotion. The despair of Oedipus is in proportion to his estimate of the blessedness of an unstained hearth, and an unpolluted hand. The horrors of the house of Pelops point the same moral; the indignation of

Antigone affords the measure of her reverence and her affection; the wrath and the remorse of Ajax gauge the value of an unblemished name; the mental agony of Neoptolemus sets faithful friendship at a higher rate than personal renown, and so forth. Take the ideas away, and neither action nor emotion would have any meaning.

The religious atmosphere is that of Greek polytheism at a transition stage. The gods are those of the popular worships, but (1) they are endowed by the poets with high symbolic meaning. Aeschylus especially, as in the 'Supplices,' the 'Agamemnon,' and the 'Prometheus,' remoulds traditional mythology with all the boldness of an original thinker; and although Sophocles innovates less in this respect, yet in him also the functions of Zeus, Apollo, and the rest are generalised and idealised, so as to be the vehicles of a truth 'more deeply interfused.' Olympus, Earth, the Aether, the Unseen are invested with a degree of awe that is the more impressive because of a vagueness of outline that is alien from the vulgar imagination. (2) The deities, like the persons of the fable, are dramatically adapted to situation, nationality, place, and time. The Theban women in the 'Septem' appeal for aid to the divinities who had the seats of their especial cults at Thebes. In the 'Agamemnon' the gratulations of the herald and of the King himself on their return are addressed to the powers who preside at Argos—the same at whose collective altar-place the daughters of Danaus had clung together like a flock of doves. And although the Theban elders in the first ' Oedipus ' direct their prayers in part to the same powers to whom Athens had looked for redemption in the time of plague, it is the Theban Artemis and the Theban Bacchus whom they particularly address. It is the son of Semele who is similarly invoked in the 'Antigone'; and in the ' Trachiniae,' where the fable is early Dorian, the oracular shrine is placed not at Delphi but at Dodona. So the prayer to Cybele in the 'Philoctetes' adds a distinct touch of local colour. Nor is it without significance, in my opinion, that in the ' Oedipus Coloneus' the guardian deities of Athens are grouped not round the Acropolis, but about the sacred precinct in which the reactionary government of the Four Hundred had been inaugurated.

In turning to Shakespeare we of course find ourselves in a wholly different intellectual atmosphere, and yet surrounded with kindred ideas and associations. For the sixteenth century the ancient conceptions of fate and of divine malignity were echoes from a distant past; familiar to the learned, for whom they were counterbalanced by Stoicism; but they had little meaning for the popular imagination. The shapes of horror which brooded over the tragic scene were of a different order. First, there were the bugbears of mediaeval superstition—Satanic influence, black arts of magic, and the prevalence

of mysterious powers of evil generally. Secondly,
terrific images of the abuse of power, of dire revenges,
of evil done by men and living after them, 'unhappy,
far-off things, and battles long ago.'

And thirdly, the mind of the age was haunted
with an apprehension of wicked policy prevailing
over innocent simplicity, associated with the great
name of Machiavelli, which had impressed his contemporaries in other lands with a vague and not
wholly unmerited fear; when the products of the
lawless Italian imagination, brought to Northern
Europe, had kindled into sombre horror the
Teutonic and Scandinavian mind. All these ideas
were still potent in the time of Marlowe. The first
is used by him with extraordinary force in the conclusion of his ' Dr. Faustus,' the second in ' Tamburlaine,' the third in ' Edward II.'; and in Shakespeare's
' Richard III.' we may still recognise the prevalence
of (2) and (3). But Shakespeare when he dared to
be himself had shaken off all in such conceptions
that was unreal. Coming face to face with the facts
of life as they surrounded him, he saw with clear
vision the nature of the struggle as one between
moral good and evil. He clearly recognised that the
dangers which assail the individual are of human
origin, though often beyond the strength of the
single will to cope withal. The ' Lucrece ' was published in 1594, when Shakespeare was thirty-one.
In spite of the fashionable prolixity, and of frigid
conceits which multiply towards the close, it sets

forth with marvellous lucidity the struggle between
lust and reason, the strife of passion with eternal
law. There is no shade of mediaeval mysticism;
all is within the purely human sphere, and yet the
moral tone is exalted far above the merely humanist
or neo-pagan level. A corrupted soul at variance
with itself, and with the innocence and truth which
it would violate, is seen in all its nakedness drawing
down upon itself, to the ruin of others, the retribution that is rendered certain by the incorruptible
fidelity and purity of her whose beauty and grace
made the temptation. The heart of the creator of
Imogen is already disclosed, and in the place of
celestial machinery we have the great personifica-
tions of Time (that 'ceaseless lackey to eternity')
and of his servant Opportunity, which give rise to a
series of generalisations showing how deeply the
poet had already reflected upon human things.

> 'Time's glory is to calm contending kings,
> To unmask falsehood, and bring truth to light,
> To stamp the seal of time in aged things,
> To wake the morn and sentinel the night,
> To wrong the wronger till he render right,
> > To ruinate proud buildings with thy hours
> > And smear with dust their glittering golden towers;
>
> 'To fill with worm-holes stately monuments,
> To feed oblivion with decay of things,
> To blot old books and alter their contents,
> To pluck the quills from ancient ravens' wings,
> To dry the old oak's sap and cherish springs,
> > To spoil antiquities of hammer'd steel
> > And turn the giddy round of Fortune's wheel;

' To show the beldam daughters of her daughter,
    To make the child a man, the man a child,
    To slay the tiger that doth live by slaughter,
    To tame the unicorn and lion wild,
    To mock the subtle in themselves beguil'd,
        To cheer the ploughman with increaseful crops,
        And waste huge stones with little water-drops.'

These and other aphorisms in which the poem
abounds come too evidently out of the fulness of the
poet's thought to warrant the suggestion that they
are commonplaces borrowed from any proverbial
philosophy whether new or old.

In 'Romeo and Juliet,' Shakespeare has left
behind him the forms of mere lyric and elegiac
poetising and has escaped from the trammels of the
chronicle or history play into the region of tragic
drama. The theme to be dramatised is the purity and
fervour of a passionate first love, which in the person
of Juliet is an entire and perfect chrysolite, and reacting upon Romeo lifts him from being a sentimental
and fantastic youth into the truest manhood. That
their passion is crossed by the strife between two
great houses, by the foolishness of their elders and
the untowardness of incalculable circumstances, belongs to the fable and to the treatment of it, which
aims at the production of awe and pity. As Professor Dowden has truly observed, the play is not
a lesson in prudential morality teaching that ' violent
delights have violent ends,'—that is the doctrine of
the Friar, whose policy in arranging the marriage

is not without *arrière pensée*. The impression left
upon the spectator, in the calm which follows the
agony of sympathetic emotion, is the fresh estimate
of the beauty, power, and tenderness of the love
of woman, which many waters cannot quench, and
which is stronger than death. Once more we are
within the human sphere. There are indeed three
references to the stars as governing human fortunes,
but they are uttered by Romeo in his distraction.
The mind of Juliet looks straight before her, never
swerving from the direct forthright. Shakespeare's
other tragedies have more both of complexity and
concentration, but he had already learned the secret
to which afterwards he gave mightier effect. If in
Juliet we have the image of a first, last, and only
love, young manhood, the too rash despairer, with
its single-minded impetuosity and scorn of circumstances, is embodied, though with less of charm, yet
with equal truth, in Romeo. There are deeper and
more complex tragic tones attending on human
passion, which Shakespeare was to develope afterwards ; meanwhile

> 'The dusky strand of Death inwoven here
> With dear Love's tie, makes Love himself more dear.'

The 'deeper tones' find their fullest expression
after the production of 'Julius Caesar.'

Tragic drama now is far from being less human,
but it is surrounded with a religious atmosphere
which comes of meditating on 'the burden of the

mystery of all this unintelligible world.' It is at once more concentrated and more comprehensive, more essentially real and at the same time more loftily ideal. Thus the process of Shakespeare's evolution may be regarded as the converse of that which we have observed in the Attic drama. Sophocles passed from the sublime vision of the eternal laws whose range is through the unclouded ether to a more purely ethical standpoint, such as appears in the 'Trachiniae,' 'Philoctetes,' and 'Oedipus Coloneus.' Shakespeare, starting from the position of a genial humanist, advanced to a more serious mood in which he contemplated life as dominated by divine law: a scheme imperfectly comprehended but bearing the impress of the Supreme Disposer.

His 'prentice hand indeed had been employed on tragedies of blood and horror, such as 'Titus Andronicus,' while his heart was elsewhere, as the poems show ; and in his first original effort he had dramatised the theme in which, as in the plays of Marlowe, the selfish love of power was represented as triumphing before its sudden fall ; but the fear of 'policy, that heretic,' had never taken a strong hold of him, and in the historical plays, from 'Richard II.' to 'Henry V.,' he treats it lightly, with supreme mastery but with ironic scorn. The cold and calculating Bolingbroke attracts him almost as little as Octavius Caesar. This is the more remarkable because the imagination of the age before and after him was

steeped in so-called Machiavellianism, as the ladder
of ambition and the key to power.

In saying that the plays from ' Hamlet ' to ' The
Tempest' and 'Cymbeline' are permeated by a religious
spirit, it is, of course, not meant that they have to
do with formal religion. It would be mistaken to
attempt to derive from them a body of dogma. In
the Roman plays the gods are those of pagan belief,
and in 'Lear' and 'Cymbeline' the spectator's thoughts
are carried into a prehistoric age; yet in all alike
there is conveyed the impression of a supreme over-
ruling law, and in 'Cymbeline ' as in ' The Tempest '
the spirit of the whole is profoundly Christian.

In the treatment of the supernatural, three elements may be noted as combined : first, a dramatic
concession to popular superstition; secondly, the
scepticism of the Renaissance regarding apparitions
as unreal mockeries ; but, thirdly, also the sense which
is Shakespeare's own that ' there are more things in
heaven and earth than are dreamt of in our philosophy,' and that human nature in its strength and
weakness is liable to influences which are ' beyond
the reaches of our souls.' It is instructive to compare the mood of Romeo in his extremity : ' Then
I defy you, stars,' with Hamlet's saying to Horatio :
' We defy augury '—' The readiness is all.'

' Poetical justice ' is of course a motive far removed from Shakespearian tragedy at its height.
It forms an element in the historical plays, where

Shakespeare, like Aeschylus, represented a young and ardent national feeling, throwing off all foreign dominion whether of Spain or of Rome, and rightly struggling not only to be free, but to exercise a world-wide sway. It is retained in 'Richard III.,' where, as in Marlowe's plays, the triumph of wickedness is counterbalanced with a final crash. It is present also in those romantic dramas with which Shakespeare closed his poetical career, but if it belongs to tragedy at all it belongs only to what Dryden has called the weaker form of tragedy, which ends happily with an earthly reconcilement : the persons and ideas opposed going off, to adopt Aristotle's comparison, as in the *dénouement* of a comedy. Mr. Courthope justly says of Massinger's moralising method : ' The moral advantage was obtained by Massinger at the expense of the highest dramatic art. In all Shakespeare's plays there is an unbroken sense of nature and reality : in Massinger, as in Beaumont and Fletcher, we are haunted by the feeling of being present at a superior puppet show, the actors in which are the mouthpieces of the poet.'

Shakespeare is not concerned, as Milton and Aeschylus were, in justifying the ways of God to man. Like Sophocles he looks steadily at the facts of life as sad experience had disclosed them. There is disillusionment, if you will, ' the sober colouring of an eye that hath kept watch o'er man's mortality ';

but the spirit which animates the whole is not to be confused with pessimism.

Mr. W. L. Courtney has well said: 'The sovereign vindication for the artist is the exceeding beauty of all human vitalities, whether they are effective or ineffective, whether they succeed or fail. It is life as such that the artist loves: strong, exuberant, magnificent life, defying laws of time and space and conquering the impossible—circumscribed indeed, if we look at its scientific conditions, but absolutely free and untrammelled in its spiritual essence. If an artist who feels the intoxication of life writes tragedies, they do not in reality depress us, because, instead of making the pulse flag and beat slower, they stir us as it were with a trumpet call, they cause the blood to flow more eagerly through our veins. Did any one ever feel his sense of vitality lowered by either reading or seeing on the stage the ruin of Othello, or the tragedy of Lear?' 'Certainly not,' we may reply, 'nor has any true-hearted person been thereby detached from the will to live.' [1]

---

[1] A louring atmosphere of pessimism seems to overhang not only the earlier but also the later forms of tragedy. In Mr. Thomas Hardy's poem of *The Dynasts*, together with some crudities, there is an unquestionably tragic vein. Lord Nelson and General Mack are genuinely tragic persons, and the scenes before and after Trafalgar are profoundly impressive. These would retain their effect if the spiritual machinery had been of a less gloomy type—if the Years had had more promise and the Earth more hope. And I venture to think that the grandeur of the poem as a work of art, and certainly its ennoblin tendency, would then have been enhanced.

Nor is the poet bent on reading to us directly any moral lesson, as if the fate of Cordelia or of Hamlet were intended to warn us against some excess of feeling or of thought. His object is to produce the peculiar pleasure which is the aim of tragedy, the pleasure of sympathetic emotion called forth by the image of an ideal sorrow. To quote once more from Mr. Courtney's 'Idea of Tragedy,' 'the law of retribution is stern enough, but there is another law that only by suffering can a man learn all the finer graces of sympathy and loving kindness flowering out of a horrible experience of evil.' That holds true in a very special sense of the mirror of suffering which is presented in tragedy, and it is in this respect that the tragic poet is a teacher. That the great spirit tried to the uttermost is accepted of the gods is what Sophocles taught through Ajax, Oedipus, Philoctetes, Electra, Antigone; that nobleness, faithfulness, and innocence have an eternal value is taught not less effectively by Shakespeare through Hamlet, Cordelia, Desdemona, Imogen.

It is ever to be borne in mind that the tragic fable as such presents the example of an exception, not of the ordinary rule. The tragic masterpieces would not move us as they do with awe and pity if both the greatness and the misfortune were not imagined as extraordinary.

Shakespeare in his moments of supreme insight

bodied forth the vision which he had made his own of 'the prophetic soul of the wide world dreaming on things to come,' and this happened to him at an epoch when, in the illumination ' of a most balmy time,'

'The sad augurs mocked their own presage
And peace proclaimed olives of endless age.'

His pen, in turning to shape such forms of things unseen, gave expression to reflections on human experience which remain an inexhaustible source of inspiration for his countrymen, and for the world at large. From this treasure-house of things new and old it is no doubt possible to extract an ethical philosophy. But to interpret him aright, each thoughtful utterance must be viewed in connection with the personality presented and with the immediate situation. Hamlet's 'pale cast of thought,' Macbeth's world-weariness, Othello's 'big wars that make ambition virtue,' Lear's 'houseless poverty,' Antony's 'Our ills told us is as our earing,' are not to be severed from their context. Only when each play is known and pondered as a whole and all are seen in reciprocal correlation are we in possession of the thought of Shakespeare; and even then the more we gain in actual experience and in the knowledge of ourselves and others, the more we are able to perceive of the profundity and boundless expansiveness of that all-embracing mind and heart.

The same is true of course of those general

maxims, those fragments of the wisdom of life, the aphoristic fruits of proverbial philosophy, which form the appropriate ornature and embroidery of tragic drama. Each owes its quota and content of truth and force to its dramatic fitness. It detracts nothing from their merit that in many, perhaps in most cases, they are derived directly, or indirectly, as the fables are, from some previous original. Mr. Churton Collins, and others before him, have collected numerous coincidences between such expressions in Shakespeare and gnômai of Greek tragedy. Striking as these resemblances are, the probability that Shakespeare drew his maxims from classic writers even through a Latin version can hardly be established, when it is considered how full the intellectual atmosphere both of writing and conversation was of such allusion, and how much of the contemporary literature, especially the literature of the stage, has perished.[1] The point to be insisted on is that whether they are reminiscences or original thoughts they arise spontaneously from the action and are not merely attached to it, or inserted. They have never in him a merely decorative effect. He is like a golfer who keeps his eye steadily upon the ball at every stroke. In reading Marlowe, or Chapman, one is often astonished

[1] Does it follow, for example, that when Dryden wrote in *Almanzor* 'There's a deaf madness in a people's fear,' he had lately been reading in Aesch. *Septem contra Thebas*, 'A people rescued knows not ruth' (*S. c. T.* 1028 τραχύς γε μέντοι δῆμος ἐκφυγὼν κακά)?

that the references to ancient and foreign writings
with which the language is brocaded should have
found acceptance from a popular audience. Such
surprises occur but seldom to the reader of Shakespeare ; but when they do so it is generally in crude
or doubtful dramas which may not be wholly his,
such as the first and second parts of 'Henry VI.' or
'Titus Andronicus': *e.g.* the expression in 'Titus
Andronicus,' I. ii. :

> 'Wilt thou draw near the nature of the gods,
> Draw near them then in being merciful '

is almost literally the same with an expression in
Cicero. That cannot be said of 'The Merchant of
Venice,' IV. i. :

> 'The quality of mercy is not strained
>
>   , ...
>
> It is an attribute of God himself,
> And earthly power doth then shew likest God's
> When mercy seasons justice,'

nor of such Scriptural allusions as, *e.g.*, 'There is a
special Providence in the fall of a sparrow.'

It happened that at about the very time when,
as we have seen, Shakespeare entered on a new
and deeper vein of ethical contemplation, Florio,
the Italian teacher, produced his English version
of the 'Essays' of Montaigne. Many parallels have
been drawn between the reflections of the French
humanist and passages in Shakespeare's mature
work, especially in 'Hamlet'; and the Utopian
views which are humorously given in 'The Tempest'

to the grave Gonzalo are almost literally transcribed from Florio. But with this exception the coincidences which have been pointed out are much the same in kind with those above referred to. That Shakespeare knew the 'Essays,' at least in their English dress, in his later years is certain, and that there was much in him akin to the genial essayist is also clear. He may have used him as Sophocles used Theognis or Simonides, but in seriousness and breadth of outlook the tragic dramatists far outwent their prototypes.

CHAPTER VI

TRAGIC CONSTRUCTION
(ἡ σύστασις τῶν πραγμάτων)

Remoulding of the fable—Evolution not contrivance—Tension and repose—Climax and catastrophe—Culmination and sequel—Tragic movement compared to a parabola—Construction in Aeschylus, Sophocles, and Shakespeare—The 'Ajax' of Sophocles—The fourth act in Shakespeare—Construction of 'Othello'—Tragic effect through accidental fatality—A possible change in the construction of 'Hamlet'—Expectation and fulfilment.

THERE is an important distinction, not always observed by commentators on Aristotle, to be made between the fable and the plot, the action being the result of both. The fable of the 'Ajax' of Sophocles is taken chiefly out of two Cyclic poems, and it is by working up this raw material with great skill of selection and adaptation that the poet has designed his plot and given shape to the action.

The fable of 'Macbeth' is drawn from Holinshed, but instead of servilely following the succession of events as in a chronicle play, the poet has woven together the circumstances of the reign of Duncan with those attending the assassination of King Duff, and has placed the murder of Macduff's wife and

children before, and not after, his rising against the
de facto monarch.

Thus pathetic poignancy is given to the motive
for the act which brings about the catastrophe. The
poet has also been led by his sense of psychological
truth, and by a sort of logic of feeling, to the original
creation of the sleep-walking scene.

Ingenuity of construction is less essential to
tragedy than to comedy. It may be said of the best
tragedies, as of the best political constitutions, that
they ' are not made, but grow,' arising naturally out
of the momentum or impetus of the emotion inherent in the main situation. Such harmony as
we find in the ' Midsummer Night's Dream ' or in
' The Merchant of Venice,' and miss in ' The Two
Gentlemen ' or in ' All's Well,' is largely matter of
contrivance ; but the word contrivance is hardly
dignified enough to characterise the ordering of the
scenes in the first ' Oedipus ' or in ' Othello,' however
appropriate it may be to such productions as those
of Heywood or Massinger. Yet, while proceeding
on simpler lines, the putting together of the
action is of high importance, and it is here that
the analogy between the handling of the fable by
Aeschylus and Sophocles on the one hand and by
Shakespeare on the other is most significant. For
it will hardly be contended that in this respect the
English poet was a conscious imitator of the Greek.

M. Jusserand has observed that the French playwright usually obeys the precept of the critic who
said : 'Let your conclusion be abrupt and simple:
resort, when you can, to the effective means of a
suddenly revealed secret.' 'D'un secret tout à coup
la vérité connue' may bring about a prompt and
interesting ending.   On the other hand Lord Tennyson is said by his biographer to have complained
that the audience of a modern play are too often
left poised on the top of a wave, 'and the wave
never breaks.' In other words, the plot increases
in intensity to the final point, whereas a great
production ought to end quietly, with (as Milton
puts it) 'all passion spent.' This peculiarity of the
later stage is noticed also by Mr. Haigh, in his
volume on 'The Tragic Drama of the Greeks,' and
he seeks to account for the difference by saying that
the ancient theatre had no curtain.   There is truth
in this, but not the whole truth.   The limits of an
art are often prescribed by outward circumstances,
but every limit is turned by great artists into an
opportunity for the creation of forms which are
instinct with an inward principle.   The *exodos* of
a Greek drama is one of its beauties ; and the
Elizabethan theatre, which likewise had no curtain,
used similar expedients for rounding off the piece
and bringing the action back into relation with the
world at large.   The speech of Malcolm at the
close of ' Macbeth,' and that of Fortinbras after the

death of Hamlet, may be cited as obvious examples. The same principle, that of ending with repose, is apparent in the most passionate masterpieces of Athenian oratory, and is accordingly formulated by Cicero in his 'Orator.' That rule was not occasioned by the absence of a curtain.

In terminology which has passed into current speech it is idle to require exactness. As Plato says, 'If you continue to be not too particular about names, you will be all the richer in wisdom. . . . The free use of words and phrases, rather than minute precision, is generally characteristic of a liberal education, and the opposite is pedantic. But,' he adds, 'sometimes precision is necessary.' And one cannot but wish that two words which are constantly employed by English writers on tragedy could be brought back to their precise and proper meaning. These words are *Climax* and *Catastrophe.*

'Climax,' meaning literally 'a ladder,' should in its secondary application properly signify *an ascent*; that is, in speaking of a drama, the rise of the action from the opening situation towards the principal crisis or turning-point; but the term in English is applied to the crisis itself. This is awkward, because no term is left for the intermediate stage of growing intensity, through which the culminating point is gradually approached.

The 'catastrophe' of a tragedy should properly signify the close of the action, which is compared to

the 'turning down' of the end of a thread in weaving.
So the word is used in classical Greek, in speaking
of an actual life; *cf.* Soph. 'Oed. Col.' 103. But
because the close of a tragic action is mostly disastrous, a 'catastrophe' in common language has
come to mean any great disaster, and in dramatic
criticism interpreters are apt to apply it to the change
of fortune which marks the critical moment of the
drama. This again is awkward, because we have no
longer any clear distinction between the principal
turning-point ($\pi\epsilon\rho\iota\pi\acute{\epsilon}\tau\epsilon\iota\alpha$) and the conclusion.

The following is what I conceive to be the formal
movement that is common to Athenian and Shakespearian tragedy. The action is carried through five
stages, corresponding roughly to the five acts of an
Elizabethan play: (1) The *Opening*, (2) The *Climax*
(or gradual ascent), (3) The *Acme* (or chief crisis),
(4) The *Sequel*, (5) The *Close*.

It is frequently assumed that a play is faulty in
which the main crisis is not held in reserve until
near the end. Such criticism is not in accordance
with the practice either of Shakespeare or of the
Attic tragic poets. In Attic tragedy the principal
change of situation, which forms the crisis of the
action, happens almost always when from one-fifth
to one-third of the drama has still to run.

What remains before the closing scene is occupied
with the development of the new situation, and of
the feelings of sympathetic awe and pity which

accompany it.   Thus it may sometimes happen that
the acme of *emotion* follows at some distance the
moment in which the *action* culminates.   In the
' Oedipus Tyrannus,' for example, the culminating
point is reached at v. 1185, where Oedipus discovers
the whole truth.   The ruin of his life is then
complete, and it is inconceivable that any more
momentous crisis can arrive to him.   But the
spectator, who is appalled by the event, has still to
realise in sympathetic emotion its full significance
and the inevitable *sequel*.   His interest from that
point onwards is not less profound, but is of a
different nature.   The tension of acute suspense
is over, and the question is not, Will the king be
ruined ? but, How will his ruin affect him ?   Gustave
Freytag speaks of this continuous movement as
pyramidal :

Gervinus would represent it as an arch, of which
the crisis forms the keystone ; and Mr. Richard
Moulton has applied this notion to Shakespeare
with an elaboration which, however ingenious
and plausible, I cannot but think to some extent
fanciful and illusory.   I should rather compare the
rise and fall of tragic intensity to a *parabola*—the
natural path of a projectile in rapid motion—of

which the *acme* lies somewhere beyond the central point.

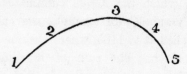

M. Francisque Sarcey, in his able critique of a performance of the ' Œdipe Roi ' at the Théâtre Français, has observed, ' Sophocle a voulu, après des émotions si terribles, après des angoisses si sèches, ouvrir la source des larmes ; il a écrit un cinquième acte.' That implies the existence of a fourth act, but I am not sure what limits this critic would assign to it. What appears to me to constitute the fourth element in the play, the *sequel* or development of the new situation, commences with the entrance of the Messenger at v. 1223, and is continued to the entrance of Creon at v. 1422.

It is in sustaining the spectator's interest at the height to which it has been raised by the arrival of the principal crisis, and in drawing forth the fund of awe and pity which that crisis has accumulated, that the power of the tragic poet is put to the severest test. The interest, however, is no longer quite the same in kind. It may be even deeper, but it is more contemplative and less attended with anxiety and excitement. When the worst is known, sympathy is no longer held in a vice, between the counter

agitations of hope and fear, but may go forth un-
restrainedly towards the hero in his misfortunes,
while it is still accompanied with awe. And in the
noblest tragedies, as in the example just adduced,
the horror of the new situation is gradually softened
with pathos.

With regard to Aeschylus the question is complicated by his use of the Trilogy. The three plays
of the 'Oresteia' are to be considered as one great
drama, whose *acme* or culminating point occurs about
v. 890 of the 'Choephori,' in the direct encounter
between Clytemnestra and her son. The chief
ascent, or *climax*, appears in the latter half of the
'Agamemnon,' which in this respect may be compared with the second act of Shakespeare's 'Macbeth'
or of his 'King Lear.' Yet in each member of
the trilogy, taken separately, there is an analogous
gradation, from the opening situation, through
agitating complications to a height of tension which
culminates before the end of the play; in the
'Agamemnon' with the death-shriek of the King
and the avowal of Clytemnestra ('Agam.' 1343-98),
in the 'Eumenides' with the acquittal of Orestes
(v. 752), nearly a fourth part of the action still
remaining.

There is an imperfect analogy between the
Aeschylean trilogy and such chronicle sequences as
the three parts of 'Henry VI.' or Schiller's 'Wallenstein,' to which last Mr. Moulton has applied the

principle in question, but the Attic play, as it was produced at one performance, has a higher unity.

If we turn now to the 'Persae,' a play of comparatively simple construction, we find that the principal change of situation comes nearly at the centre of the play. It is actually complete at v. 597 when the Persian Elders have lamented over the defeat of Salamis. But the effect of this great reverse is only fully realised when the ghost of Darius is evoked from the shades. His apparition at v. 680 is the culminating point or *acme* of the drama; the sequel or development of the new situation is formed by the colloquy between Darius, Atossa, and the Elders, extending to v. 851. The sympathetic interest of the spectators is continuously deepened, but is calmer and less agitating than the impression produced by the narrative of the defeat, and it melts into pathos at the end of the play. The last stasimon, in which the Elders dwell upon the glory that is departed, divides that impressive colloquy from the entrance of Xerxes and the lamentation between him and the Elders, which constitutes the close.

In the development of the altered situation there may occur a new period of suspense—a knot to be resolved—a δέσις followed by a λύσις. But such a crisis is secondary and subordinate to the main action. Thus in the 'Trachiniae' the change of fortune is completed at v. 820, with the exit of Deianira

after the narrative of Hyllus. But there still remain
doubts to be resolved. Will Heracles in his agony
ascertain the truth? What effect will it produce on
him, and what will be the final scene? The fourth
act, as I should call it, consisting of the nurse's
narrative, the entrance of the suffering Heracles, his
long rhesis, and the colloquy between him and his
son, forms not the least impressive portion of the
play, and leads up to the *close* or 'catastrophe' in
the preparations for the funeral pyre. But the *acme*
of intense expectancy is past, and a new situation
has been created, when once the effect of the poison
has been described by Hyllus and understood by
Deianira.

Similarly, after the exit of Creon at v. 1114 of the
'Antigone,' when his resolution has been broken down
by the prophecy of Teiresias, a new state of suspense
arises, as to what the *sequel* will be.

Will the maiden be released in time? Will
Polynices have due burial? These doubts are solved
by the report of the Messenger, and the death of
Eurydice is still in reserve. Tragic interest is thus
maintained at a high point until the close, where the
remorse of Creon is complete. But all this forms the
development of the situation which has been produced
by the sentence on Antigone. The drama really
culminates in the second rhesis of Teiresias, vv.
1064–1090. Similarly, the recall of Othello, and the
massacre of Macduff's wife and children, are new

incidents attendant on the sequel and pointing
forward to the catastrophe.

It is with respect to this very principle of climax
and dramatic movement that the ' Ajax ' of Sophocles
has been severely criticised, and in my judgment
inadequately defended. Mr. Haigh writes as follows
in the work already cited : 'The construction of the
" Ajax " varies in point of merit. In the first part
of the play the preparation for the crisis is admirably
contrived ; and the deception of Tecmessa and the
Chorus, and their extravagant joy at the hero's
supposed recovery, intensify the effect of the catastrophe which immediately follows. But after the
death of Ajax, as the scholiast pointed out, there is
an end of the tragic interest ; and the final scenes,
with their protracted wrangling over the disposal of
the body, are frigid by comparison. No doubt the
subject of burial was one of supreme importance
to the ancients ; but this fact hardly justifies the
excessive length of the concluding dialogues. Nor
can it be contended that their object was to re-
habilitate the character of the national hero, which
had been exhibited in a dishonourable light at the
beginning of the play, by giving Teucer an opportunity of extolling his achievements. The reputation
of Ajax had already been sufficiently redeemed by
the impressive dignity of his final appearance. It
is simpler to suppose, with the scholiast, that as
the subject of the tragedy was deficient in incident,

Sophocles chose to fill it out to the necessary length
with one of those rhetorical contests in which the
ancients delighted. At the same time, the debate
was one which would gratify the national pride of
the Athenians. Teucer, who might be regarded as
the representative of Athens, was seen maintaining
a successful contest with the two great heroes of the
Peloponnesus, and his invectives against Spartan
arrogance would be certain to rouse the enthusiasm of
the Athenian audience. But it must be admitted that
scenes of this kind, though effective upon the stage,
fall below the usual level of Sophoclean tragedy.'

Sir R. C. Jebb, in the introduction to his edition
of the 'Ajax,' pp. xxviii, xxix, writes as follows upon
the same subject: 'If the sequel to the hero's death
is to be justified as a subject of dramatic art, it has
to be explained how the action of the play, from
beginning to end, can be regarded as an organic
whole. The idea which pervades it, giving it unity
and coherence, must be such that the death of Ajax
can be viewed, not as a catastrophe, after which
everything else becomes tame, but rather as a tragic
event necessarily leading to the events which follow
it, so that the true climax is reached only in that
decision which rescues the corpse of Ajax from dishonour.' *Ibid.* p. xxxii: 'The veto upon the burial
of Ajax is an inevitable consequence of his action,
and one for which the spectator has been prepared ;
so that the latter part of the play is not an arbitrary

addition to the former, but a natural, indeed a necessary, development of it. Secondly, this veto raises an issue still more momentous, for Athenians, than the question whether Ajax is to live or die—viz. the issue whether he is or is not to attain the sanctity of a hero. Hence the true climax of the play is not his death, but the decision that he shall be buried.'

I will not cavil at the use made by either author of the terms which I discussed at first. Both clearly use *catastrophe* to mean the principal change of fortune, and Sir R. C. Jebb, in accordance with common use, means by *climax* the *acme* of tragic interest. In finding this towards the *close* of the ' Ajax ' he differs from Mr. Haigh and from the scholiast. Few who have followed the drama attentively throughout will immediately and unreservedly subscribe to what cannot but seem to them a paradoxical judgment. But are Mr. Haigh and others therefore justified in their condemnation of the later portion of the play? Not if the view maintained in this chapter is the right one. The error on both sides lies in looking for the point of keenest interest towards the end of the drama. With all that Sir R. C. Jebb has said in defence of the unity and coherence of the ' Ajax ' I heartily agree. As he well puts it, the latter part of the play is not an arbitrary addition to the former, but a natural, indeed a necessary, development of it. It is the development of the new situation which has been created by the hero's death. That

has called forth a tide of emotion, which does not
subside at once; the highest wave of the τρικυμία is
not immediately followed by smooth waters. But
no subsequent event can arouse a fresh agitation
to equal the effect of this. Even in the presence
of his brother's corpse Teucer cannot produce an
impression to surpass, or even to rival, that which
Ajax has made, any more than Macduff's 'noble
passion' can excite the audience equally with
Macbeth's distraction in the banquet scene. But
Teucer can deepen the impression already made. He
can infix and drive it home, and with the pathetic
figure of Tecmessa, with the child Eurysaces, who
is heir to Salamis, and the grand moderation of
Odysseus, contrasted as it is with the insensate
violence of the Atreidae, Teucer can be the centre of
a series of dramatic scenes well calculated to keep
alive the profound emotions which have been excited
by the main action. And that, as I maintain, is the
true function of the concluding portion of a great
tragedy, the part answering to the fourth and fifth
acts of such Elizabethan dramas as 'Macbeth,'
'Othello,' or 'King Lear.''

Shakespeare is taken to task on this very ground
by nineteenth-century critics, who have observed that
the *action* of his tragedies is apt to culminate about
the end of the third act. They are aware that
Romeo's banishment, the flight of Brutus and
Cassius, Hamlet's departure for England after the

closet scene, the apparition of Banquo, the forced
removal to Dover of King Lear, and the disaster at
Actium, mark the crises or turning-points of the
several dramas to which these incidents belong, and
Shakespeare is accordingly 'sent to the barber's'
with Polonius's beard.[1] The poet's art in sustaining
our emotional sympathies through the scenes that
follow, of riveting attention upon the new situation
which the main action has created, and causing the
spectator's thoughts to hang with unabated interest
upon the inevitable descent and close, is ill appreciated by modern audiences, who are impatient of
longueurs.

An exception is made, however, in favour of
'Othello,' and by this classical example the thesis
which has been defended in the present article is
thought to be manifestly rebutted. For where is
the *acme* of that great tragedy, if not in the
violent death of Desdemona? I willingly admit,
or rather I am ready to maintain, that in that final
scene the *emotion* of the spectator is called forth in
the fullest volume, and has mounted to an intensity
of intolerable poignancy. To read aloud beyond the
words, 'I have no wife,' without breaking down,
argues either insensibility or a rare control of feeling.
But the supreme skill with which this effect is produced has been rendered the more possible because
the *action* of the play, in the strict sense of the

[1] See *National Review* of December 1888, p. 493.

word, has already culminated.   The acme or turning-
point was reached, all doubt had been resolved, the
end was determined, from the moment when Iago's
triumph was assured and the poison of jealousy had
saturated the soul of Othello.   Consider the position
of the spectator at three cardinal points in the
latter portion of the play :

(1) Act III. sc. iii. lines 446–448—

> 'All my fond love thus do I blow to Heaven.
> 'Tis gone.
> Arise, black vengeance, from the hollow hell,'

and to the end of the scene.

(2) Act IV. sc. i. line 252—

> '*Oth.* Devil !
> *Des.* I have not deserved this.'

(3) Act V. sc. ii.

> 'It is the cause, it is the cause, my soul—'

the whole scene.

(1) At the first of these three points the spectator who has followed with intense anxiety the
prolonged agony of doubt in Othello is finally
certified of the fatality in store, and henceforward
awaits with awestruck apprehension the inevitable
sequel.

(2) The second point is handled with supreme
judgment.   The arrival of the commissioners from
Venice with the bitter news that he is superseded
by Cassio touches Othello to the quick, and provokes

a violent outburst of the uncontrollable passion which is ripe within him; and this exhibition of his distemperature is aggravated by the unsuspecting simplicity, or, if you will, by the innocent stupidity, of Desdemona.

(3) Othello's passion has its final outgoing in the scene which forms the true catastrophe. But how it has become calmed and sublimated, steadied as it were, by brooding over its own depth!

> ' I know not where is that Promethean spark
> That can thy light relume.'

That is not the tone which suits the acme of a tragic action. It marks the full development of the *sequel*; and in the hero's despair, when undeceived too late, there is the same element of preternatural outward tranquillity.

> ' Soft you, a word or two before you go . . .'

Already in that speech the larger light of day breaks in upon the stage, and we are reminded that this private grief is but an incident in a world-wide history :

> ' This wide and universal theatre
> Presents more woeful pageants than the scene
> Wherein we play in.'

The concluding speech of Lodovico is herein analogous to that of Malcolm in ' Macbeth,' of Fortinbras in ' Hamlet,' of Albany in ' Lear,' of Octavius Caesar in ' Antony and Cleopatra,' or those of Antony and Octavius in ' Julius Caesar.'

Such 'rounding off,' restoring the spectator to himself and to the world, is in accordance with the 'ending with repose' which was recommended to the orator by Cicero. But the conclusion ought not to be brought in too suddenly, lest tragic depth should be extenuated and tragic pathos weakened or nullified. And on this account, as the author of 'Cyrano' has perceived, and as Sophocles, according to M. Sarcey, was aware, the addition of a fifth act was justified. Especially is this the case in dramas which, to use John Dryden's happy phrase, have a 'double turn'; as, for example, the 'Philoctetes' of Sophocles and several plays of Euripides. If the action closes with reconciliation, or with any softening of the tragic mood, great care should be taken that the main effect should not be impaired. This is successfully achieved in the 'Oedipus Coloneus,' but not, I venture to think, in the 'Philoctetes,' where the impressiveness of the psychological struggle is decidedly enfeebled by the intervention of Heracles from the sky. As Aristotle says of a similar ending, the persons who have been seen in a deadlock of contention go off arm in arm (so to speak), as in the winding up of a comedy.

The completeness of tragic effect is sometimes secured by a minute arrangement which is due to the invention of the poet. Thus the catastrophe in 'King Lear' depends on the delay of Edmund's confession and the pre-occupations which for the moment have absorbed the attention of Albany. In 'Romeo and Juliet' Friar Laurence's good intention is baulked by the external accident which frustrates the errand of Friar John. So in the 'Trachiniae' of Sophocles, Hyllus, being engrossed with attending to his father, learns all too late the innocence of Deianira's act. And in the 'Antigone' it is obvious that if the release of the maiden had preceded the burial of Polynices, as the Elders had advised, the final disaster might have been avoided. Sir Richard Jebb regards this as a flaw in construction, which he attributes to the rhetorical motive of providing for a climax in the report of the Messenger. But surely in any case the intention is tragic and not merely rhetorical, nor can it be admitted to detract from the soundness of the perfect piece if we appreciate rightly the character of Creon. The chorus of Elders, although curbing their voices to the tyrant's sway, partook somewhat of the public sympathy for the heroic maiden, but when Creon's resolution is broken down he is not moved by any human tenderness or compunction, but by the fear of the gods, and of the evils which Teiresias has prophesied as threatening the State.

Tragic intensity calls for some relief, and part of the dramatist's skill is shown in his manner of interposing pauses in the action. From the large scale on which Shakespeare works, and also from the practice of the contemporary stage, such flat places are more considerable in him. In the first 'Oedipus,' the King's narrative to Jocasta before the entrance of the Corinthian has something of the same effect as Hamlet's colloquy with the players. The action may be said *reculer pour mieux sauter*; but it is more frequently in the development of the sequel, corresponding to the fourth act of the English play, that the dramatic movement is felt to linger for a while. The poet has sufficient faith in the volume of sympathy which he has called forth to interpose a pause without fearing that emotion will subside. The reclamations of the two generals in the 'Ajax' afford such a stopping-place, and the transition to the English court in 'Macbeth,' with the voluminous speech by which Malcolm tries the faith of Macduff, may be excused on this ground. The audience enjoy a brief respite while the change is being prepared from horror to pity. The grave-diggers in 'Hamlet' exercise a corresponding function.

Some of the best interpreters complain of tediousness in the fourth act of a Shakespearian drama, and it may be that in 'Macbeth' he has followed Holinshed too closely, and that in 'Lear' the difficulty of adjusting plot and underplot has encumbered his method. The fact remains that in this mode of treatment he differs from his predecessors and successors, while he agrees, unconsciously

as I believe, with the great masters of antiquity.
Other dramatic poets, like Ford in 'The Broken
Heart,' instead of developing the sequel of the
precedent action, have recourse to fresh incidents
and complications by way of creating fresh excitement, but in doing so have injured the harmony of
their work and blunted the keenness of the impression.
The emotions that have been raised to the height
by the death of Ajax, or the condemnation of
Antigone, have a fulness in them that is only drawn
out and magnified through the following scenes,
and those who have witnessed the passion of
Macbeth at the apparition of Banquo are prepared
to realise the depth of wickedness into which he
falls, with the consequent world-weariness; to be
moved aright by the grief of Macduff, and feel due
satisfaction at his revenge.—It must be admitted,
however, that the insertion from Holinshed of the
English doctor and the King's evil, probably due to
the popular wish to flatter James I., is a serious
interruption of the dramatic movement.—The
totality of impression thus conveyed is a far greater
thing than the sudden despair of Dr. Faustus, or of
Richard III., or the death of Calantha in 'The
Broken Heart'; or, again, than such accumulation
of agony as Webster produced in his 'Duchess of
Malfi.' With Shakespeare's best comedies the case
is different, for there the feelings to be excited are
of a lighter kind. Thus 'The Merchant of Venice'

culminates with the trial scene which forms the fourth act of that harmonious drama. Another way in which the gradual descent from the main crisis or turning-point is made is through the development of a subordinate action, as in Heywood's ' A Woman Killed by Kindness,' perhaps the most perfect of domestic tragedies. And in melodrama and tragi-comedy, where the volume of emotion is comparatively exiguous, the crisis is naturally delayed, and the *dénouement* takes the form of a surprise—as in Ford's 'Lover's Melancholy.'

The transposition of scenes is a well-known cause of corruption in the playhouse copies. A noted example is the state of the text in the tragedy of ' Sir Thomas More ' ; and it may therefore be doubted whether the peculiarity in this respect of the First Quarto of 'Hamlet' belongs to Shakespeare's first draft or to a corruption of this nature. The following is the difference in question : In the First Quarto, the suggestion of Corambis, *i.e.* Polonius, that his daughter should be thrown in Hamlet's way whilst he and the King should watch their interview unseen, is immediately followed by Hamlet's solitary entrance, the soliloquy ' To be or not to be,' and the painful interview with Ophelia. Next comes the scene with Polonius, the mystification of Rosencrantz and Guildenstern, the arrival of the players and the soliloquy ' Oh what a rogue and peasant slave am I.' Then follows Rosencrantz's

and Guildenstern's report to the King, Hamlet's
advice to the players, his conversation with Horatio,
and the play scene.

In the Second Quarto, as in our copies, the talk
with Polonius, the conversation with Rosencrantz
and Guildenstern, and the entrance of the players
leading up to 'What's Hecuba to him?', also the
report of the false friends to the King, come before
and not after the great soliloquy and the agonising
scene with Ophelia. This last is followed almost
immediately by the play scene, only prefaced by
Hamlet's advice to the players, in his anxiety that
his own lines should be well spoken, and, while they
are dressing for performance, his confidential talk
with Horatio at this the crisis of his fate.

The change, if change it is, is greatly for the
better. How much more significant is the calm
utterance of deep melancholy, and the poignant
enforced interview with his lost love, awakening an
agony of wounded affection and suspicion, at the
moment when the fateful issue is about to be
determined, when the cardinal discovery is impending, and the need for crushing out 'all pressures
past' is more than ever imperative in its demand!
That at this moment, when the great wave of
emotion is at point to break, he should have so
clear a proof of the frailty of the reed on which
his heart once leant, is tragic indeed! And the
brooding calm of meditation is 'the torrent's

smoothness ere it dash below.' The 'rogue and peasant slave' soliloquy, on the other hand, is in a mood of passion which suits the rising intensity of the action, rather than its height. It corresponds with the dagger soliloquy in 'Macbeth,' or the meeting with Regan and Goneril before Gloster's castle, rather than with the apparition of Banquo or the storm upon the heath, the hovel and the remove to Dover.

In another point of great importance the editions are at fault, and this perhaps indicates that Act III. is unusually prolonged (but not more so than in other plays of the period, for instance, in 'Edward III.'). The partition between Acts III. and IV., which has no authority either in the Quartos or Folios, appears to have been made in the editions with more regard to the length than to the substance. The natural division seems to be after the words in the fourth scene of Act IV., 'My thoughts be bloody or be nothing worth.' For a great and significant pause is interposed by Hamlet's voyage to England, and the effect of this break in continuity is obscured by the present arrangement. From his exit after the line above quoted, Hamlet is absent from the court, and, for most of the time, from Denmark. The interval is occupied by Ophelia's mad scenes, her death, and the return of Laertes, of which Hamlet has hitherto been unaware. For the moment his thoughts have been withdrawn from

the immediate scene of his troubles, and the frustration of his schemes, and his mind has wandered
to a calm, though sombre, contemplation of human
things. This aloofness, as I may call it, would be
presented with greater force if the acts were divided
in the manner I have indicated. In the graveyard,
besides the vein of brooding speculation, Hamlet's
detachment from present things is shown by his
reminiscence of Yorick, recalling former days in
his father's brilliant court. From this reverie, he
is suddenly roused by hearing the name of Ophelia.
His old love instantly bursts into flame, and he
asserts more right in her than forty thousand
brothers. He knows not that Laertes' mind has been
poisoned against him, and he immediately repents of
the towering passion which meanwhile has confirmed the evil purpose of Laertes, and has sealed
the doom of both men. That completes the *change*
which forms a proper consummation of the fourth
act.

'Expectation is less aesthetic than fulfilment'
is the true saying of a recent critic, anticipated by
Coleridge, and in a Shakespearian or Sophoclean
drama the impression produced by the evolution of
the sequel is not less deep because the tension of
suspense has been relaxed. In the acting of 'Julius
Caesar' the quarrel of the two generals in Brutus'
tent is more effective even than the oration of

Antony.   But if regarded as a tragedy, and not
merely as a Roman historical play, the effect of the
climax is impaired, because Brutus, who is really the
protagonist, appears to disadvantage in Act III.,
where his personality is eclipsed by the brilliant
appearance of Antony.

CHAPTER VII

TRAGIC DICTION

Natural and artificial grammar—Special causes of difficulty in
the interpretation of tragedy—Remote analogies between the
language of Shakespeare and that of Sophocles.

WE have not yet done with the definition of
Aristotle. There is a clause in it which is sometimes passed over too lightly. Although tragic
drama is 'enacted and not merely reported,' it is
also true that it is 'enacted through language,' and
the language is 'embellished,' investing pity with
sublimity and horror with beauty. Every word,
every single intonation as originally conceived by
the poet must pass immediately from the heart of
the performer to the heart of the audience, if the
work is to have its entire and legitimate effect.
This truth appears to be ignored by those who
labour at producing Greek dramas in the original
before a non-classical audience, or who, without
knowing foreign languages, frequent performances
of plays in French or German, Dutch or Italian.
And the actor, unless he is of that rare kind whose
ambition is to interpret a great poet, is apt to

magnify his function, as if the words mattered little, and action helped out with scenery were all in all.

Mr. Sidney Walker, in his ' Critical Examination ' (§ 3), called attention to the difference which exists between ' natural and artificial grammar.' In all languages there is in fact a continual transition from the one to the other. The most primitive modes of expression have laws of their own, from which reflection afterwards deduces grammatical rules ; but there is a vast difference between the spontaneous use of speech and the self-conscious regulation of it. The style of M. Jourdain, before and after his discovery that he spoke in prose, could hardly be the same. A curious example of such alteration in one particular appears in Dryden's revision of his ' Essay on Dramatic Poetry,' where—sometimes with cumbrous effect—he persistently rejects the employment of the preposition in *anastrophe* which he had been *addicted to*, or rather, *to which he had been addicted.* (See the selection of Dryden's prose writings by Prof. W. P. Ker.)

Yet even in a highly developed state of the grammatical consciousness, some natural irregularities are liable to recur. I once tried to convince Professor Huxley that a sentence in his monograph on Hume—' No event is too extraordinary to be impossible '—involved a solecism. But with characteristic combativeness he defended it as ' idiomatic.' I have never been able to ascertain whether the late Dr. Kennedy, who accused a certain interpreter of ' undue exaggeration,' would or would not have justified the pleonastic expression as attributable to unusual emotion.

The controversy which gave rise to such ' emotion ' in the breast of an eminent philologer turned on what I still venture to think a real set of phenomena in a transitional phase of the literary use of language in ancient Greece. And the question is one on which the last word has hardly yet been spoken. It is treated on both sides with greater moderation : but when certain limits are transgressed, Dr. Kennedy's successors in verbal scholarship, while avoiding his truculence, and endeavouring after ' gentle treatment,' can with difficulty disguise their contempt.

The fact is undeniable that, roughly speaking, for one place in Homer or Plato (not' to mention Lysias or Xenophon) where the meaning may be disputed, there are twenty such in Aeschylus or Sophocles and ten in Euripides. Many scholars appear to be satisfied with a brief and facile way of accounting for this inequality. They are contented with saying that the tragic texts are exceptionally corrupt. And some will praise the logical clearness and grammatical coherency of the great masters, which is to be restored to them for our benefit by the certainty of conjecture. But the explanation only suggests new difficulties. For if this logical and grammatical perfection were so transparent and so indubitably recoverable, how came it ever to be lost? What led the scribes, who have preserved for us with comparative faithfulness the deepest thoughts of Plato, to make such havoc of the tragedians, if the language of those great poets was such as no reader could fail to understand? This difficulty is not met by the hypothesis of 'playhouse interpolation.' For if our present copies corresponded to those authorised for performance even in late classical times, we should not for that reason expect them to err on the side of obscurity. Nor does any theory of subsequent corruptions account for the significant fact that the meaning of Aeschylus was in dispute amongst the contemporaries of Aristophanes.

It may be not altogether idle if, as a preliminary step, we try (as Plato might say) to 'take hold of the matter as a whole'; i.e. to consider whether there may not be some kinds of difficulty which are inherent in the language, not only of Greek tragedy, but of serious dramatic writing generally. Analogies are not necessarily unreal because remote—as the repeated comparison of Sophocles with Virgil is enough to show—and great tragedy has been so rare that, however diverse may have been the conditions of its two greatest moments, we may fairly look for points of correlation between them.

Confining our attention to linguistic difficulties

for the present, one thing is certain. The English reader of Shakespeare in the nineteenth century (it was still more so in the eighteenth) requires to be ' edified by the margent ' far more frequently than the reader of Spenser or Bacon.

Now the text of Shakespeare is allowed to be by no means pure ; but the fact here stated would remain even if all the passages annotated by Dyce were left out of view. Of ten fairly educated persons taken at a venture, how many could paraphrase at sight without hesitation or error a soliloquy of Hamlet or Macbeth, or even a speech of Portia or Bassanio ? Many lines which no competent editor has suspected of corruption are yet by no means clear to the average reader nowadays. And yet Shakespeare must have been intelligible to his own contemporaries. This apparent anomaly becomes less strange when it is considered that the language of dramatic poetry is necessarily (1) idiomatic, (2) condensed, (3) helped out by action.

(1) The dramatic poet, in virtue of his function, stands nearer to the living language of men than any other literary artist. In giving form to his creations, he must continually draw afresh from the running waters of vernacular speech, with which his work has a direct vital relation. His business is to imitate human language, not as written, but as spoken, and the material which he thus borrows he must fuse again with the intensity and subtilty of

ideal emotion before he can find an appropriate vehicle for his conceptions. Here are two great factors, which must both be recognised—the spontaneous, instinctive fancy which gives its stamp to current parlance, and the refining influence of poetic feeling—two elements which are obviously distinct, yet whose operations it is difficult, and for a remote period well-nigh impossible, adequately to discriminate. For example, the use of the preposition ' of ' with abstract substantives to denote an attribute was manifestly a conversational idiom in the time of Shakespeare. Yet in employing it so frequently as he does, he may have had a literary motive. This is less clear, however, than the fact, which is most in point, that for the modern reader this habit (whether of ' idiom ' or ' idiotism ') has thrown some obscurity over such lines as :

> ' And thus do we of wisdom and of reach,
> With windlasses and with assays of bias—'

> ' That makes calamity of so long life.'

> ' And in a pass of practice
> Requite him for your father.'

The subjunctive mood was more used then than now, but in such passages as 'Hamlet' I. ii. 17, ' Julius Cæsar' III. i. 159, 'The Merchant of Venice' III. ii. 20, there is a specially Shakespearian turn, which is not always caught by the intelligent reader. See below, Chapter VIII. pp. 113, 114.

This point, in its relation to Greek tragedy, has been lately treated independently by two scholars of marked ability, Dr. W. G. Rutherford and Mr. A. W. Verrall. Dr. Rutherford in an introductory chapter of his ' New Phrynichus ' has argued forcibly in favour of the theory that the so-called Ionic element in tragedy is really a ' survival ' from the earlier spoken dialect of Attica. This bears out the conception of Herodotus, that the Attic people were simply a branch of the Ionic race, differing from the rest only in having retained their first seats, and in their possession of national and political liberty. Mr. Verrall, on the contrary, lays stress on the other element, that of artistic refinement, and, in the lyrical portions of the tragic drama especially, would account for coincidences with earlier literature, and for other peculiarities, by the poet's effort to give beauty to his work through subtilties of association.

I would suggest that both factors, the vernacular and the literary, may have been operative. And while the attempt at assigning to either its due value would be the work of a ' laborious and not too fortunate man,' the fact as generally stated is sufficient for the present purpose.

(2) Only it should be remembered that *refinement* in tragedy runs mainly in the direction of *condensation*. For in the idealisation of emotion concentration and intensity are all-important. Those who had the high satisfaction of seeing Salvini's Lear

cannot fail to have observed, if they consulted the
libretto, how the speeches were inevitably lengthened
in transferring them to Italian. (And if any one
attempted to express in other words (say) the
soliloquy of Macbeth beginning 'If it were done,
when 'tis done,' the paraphrase, if approximately
adequate, would be much longer than the original.

Once more (3) in dramatic writing the language
is only one amongst several conjoint modes of expression, and even of the language the written
words are only a part.   Plays are made to be acted,
not merely to be read; it is no cause for wonder,
therefore, if they lose something, not only of their
effect, but of their meaning, for the cursory reader.
When Portia says to Bassanio,

> 'That only to stand high *in your account*,
> I might in beauties, virtues, livings, friends,
> Exceed account,'

the superficial reader is apt to understand 'in your
esteem.'   But those who have seen a worthy Portia
and heard her tones, cannot fail to know, with every
deeper student, that her wish is that she may constitute an important 'asset' amongst her husband's
possessions.

An error which the liveliness of action should
obviate, though it is natural in the closet-student, is
to read in 'Twelfth Night,' II. ii. 15, 'She took *no*
ring of me,' for 'She took the ring of me.'   When
the scene is realised, the reasons in favour of the

older reading, though even Dyce pronounced them over-subtle, must commend themselves as simple and natural. The fine sisterly tact of Viola, who will not give Olivia away to her steward, and the poverty of the repetition when (if ' *no* ring' is read) she afterwards observes to herself what she has just said to another, are then too obvious to be missed.

In 'King John,' IV. ii. 233, many students have no doubt concurred with Dyce, who in his second edition reads '*And* turned an eye of doubt upon my face.' To make '*As*' in the traditional reading bear the force of '*As much as to*' seems to them ' impossibly harsh.' But no one who has tried to realise the speech, even in dramatic recitation, can fail to see that a fine point is missed, or rather spoiled, by the new reading.

The words used by Milton in contrasting the study of poetry with that of logic and philosophy are applicable to tragic poetry in the highest degree. And all Greek poetry is 'more simple, sensuous, and passionate,' not only as compared with logic, but also with oratory. It has, indeed, a logic of its own, if the term be not inappropriate to the expression of feeling. And it has also a rhetoric of its own. But this rhetoric is more condensed and passionate than the rhetoric of the agora.

To gauge the difference between rhetorical and dramatic eloquence, it is only necessary to glance at the third act of ' Julius Caesar,' perhaps the most

effective *representation* of successful oratory in the
compass of dramatic literature. Yet how much is
there which, in the actual oration, would have been
differently put ? At how many points would ex-
pansion have taken the place of concentration,
breadth of refinement; repetition, recapitulation,
preluding—that of subtle transition? Might not
Antony's topics have furnished forth a speech of
three hours or sixty pages ? Are the words,

> 'Now lies he there,
> And none so poor to do him reverence,'

turned or arranged as the speaker would have
arranged and turned them ?

In suggesting the existence of remote analogies
between the language of Shakespeare and that of
certain portions of the Greek drama, I do not forget
the great difference, not only in language, but in
form and structure, between the masterpieces of the
ancient and the modern world. The idioms and
modes of thought are different, the means of condensation are different, the conditions of representation are widely different ; the strain of feeling is as
different as the imagery through which it is conveyed. But the truth remains, and has an important
bearing on interpretation, that Greek tragedy, no
less than English, is idiomatic, concentrated, made
to be acted more than read, and, above all, simple,
sensuous, and passionate.

We might thus proceed to formulate a series of

'*canons*' which, although less easy of mechanical application than those of Dawes, are in no degree less certain. 'The language of tragedy,' we might say, 'is (1) idiomatic, (2) condensed and pregnant, (3) histrionic and dramatic, (4) simple, (5) sensuous (*i.e.* picturesque and figurative), and (6) impassioned.'

CHAPTER VIII

TRAGIC DICTION—*continued*

Tragic diction in Shakespeare and Sophocles is (1) idiomatic;
(2) concentrated; (3) dramatic; (4) simple; (5) sensuous (*i.e.*
vivid, not prosaic); (6) passionate (*i.e.* emotional, not frigid).

I PROCEED to exemplify the points put forward in
the preceding chapter, with reference to the text
and interpretation (I.) of Shakespeare, and (II.) of
Sophocles.

Tragic diction, then, is

(1) *Idiomatic.* Diction that is natural and expressive is preferred to that which is grammatically
precise.

Any reader of Shakespeare who examines closely
the language of 'The Tempest,' *e.g.* Act I. sc. ii.,
will find it bristling with anacolutha; yet these are
hardly felt in a cursory perusal, except perhaps
lines 99–102,

> 'Like one,
> Who having, into truth, by telling of it,
> Made such a sinner of his memory,
> To credit his own lie.'

Emphasis through negation, the subtlest of all
sources of fallacy, often leads to some disturbance

of language.　Sometimes this merely occasions obscurity, as in ' King Lear,' I. i. 5–7 :

' Equalities are so weighed that curiosity in neither can make choice of either's moiety '—

Or in ' Cymbeline,' I. i. 1 :

　　　　　' Our bloods
No more obey the Heavens than our courtiers
Still seem as does the King ' ;

i.e. ' Our courtiers' looks reflect the King's countenance as surely as our bodily condition is influenced by the state of the sky.'

More often some complication of negatives results in an illogical expression.

' Macbeth,' III. vi. 8 :

　　　' Who cannot want the thought how monstrous
　　　It was for Malcolm and for Donalbain
　　　To kill their gracious father ? '

On this Malone observes that Shakespeare was careless of ' such minutiae.'

More singular is the occasional confusion of ' less ' with ' more.'

' Coriolanus,' I. iv. 13 :

　　　　' Tullus Aufidius, is he within your walls ?
1*st Sen.* No, nor a man that fears you less than he,
　　　　That's lesser than a little.'

' Winter's Tale,' III. ii. 55–6 :

　　　　　　' I ne'er heard yet
　　　That any of these bolder vices wanted
　　　Less impudence to gainsay what they did
　　　Than to perform it first.'

'Cymbeline,' I. iv. 24 :

> 'For taking a beggar without less quality.'

These passages make it plain that in 'As You Like It,' V. iv. 154 :

> 'Even daughter welcome in no less degree,'

the meaning is 'Not even a daughter could be more welcome,' and that by punctuating after 'daughter,' as is commonly done, the naturalness of the expression is impaired. Where a triple negative is involved, one is apt to be dropped out (compare the Greek οὐ μόνον for οὐ μόνον οὔ) :

'Coriolanus,' I. ii. 19 :

> 'Nor did you think it folly
> To keep your great pretences veiled till when
> They needs must show themselves.'

i.e. 'Nor did you think it folly *not* to.'

Mr. H. Bradley, in his 'Making of English,' observes that the Elizabethans had the use of moods which are now obsolete. Shakespeare's use of these is not always easy to analyse ; for instance, in 'Hamlet,' I. ii. 17, the words 'Now follows that you know,' *i.e.* 'the next thing is for you to be informed that,' are often misunderstood as if 'know' were in the indicative ; and it might puzzle even a Board school scholar to parse 'Julius Caesar,' III. i. 159 :

> 'Live a thousand years,
> I shall not find myself so apt to die— '

or 'The Merchant of Venice,' III. ii. 20 :

> 'Prove it so,
> Let Fortune go to Hell for it not I.'

See also 'The Tempest,' II. i. 228: 'If heed me'; II. i. 267 : 'Keep in Tunis.'

Nouns also are sometimes out of construction, as in 'The Tempest,' I. ii. 147 :

> 'Nor tackle, sail, nor mast.'

A similar breviloquentia occurs in 'Macbeth,' III. i. 131 :

> 'Always thought
> That I require a clearness.'

where the participial clause is absolute.

A glance at Furniss' Variorum edition is enough to show how often the grammatical sense of interpreters, especially in the eighteenth century, has stumbled over slight irregularities of idiom. Thus, in 'Macbeth,' II. ii. 55, the slight enallage in 'Tarquin's ravishing strides' (*i.e.* the strides of the ravisher Tarquin) led Johnson to conjecture 'With Tarquin ravishing, slides toward his design.'

In Greek, of course, the duplication of the negative has passed into a grammatical rule. But the practice is not quite invariable, at least in tragedy. Thus in Sophocles 'Oed. Col.' 277–8 :

> καὶ μὴ θεοὺς τιμῶντες εἶτα τοὺς θεοὺς
> μοίραις ποιεῖσθε μηδαμῶς,

whatever reading is adopted, the negatives are independent of each other; and on the other hand the

common idiom is extended to places where one of
the negatives is only implied. Thus in 'Oed. Tyr.'
57 :

ἔρημος ἀνδρῶν μὴ ξυνοικούντων ἔσω,

it is a mistake to punctuate after ἔρημος.

In 'Oed. Tyr.' 1463-4, where the negative is
repeated with an inversion, this change, which has
caused some difficulty, has really a pathetic effect :
'With regard to whom my table was never served
apart (that they should feed) away from me.'

Some scholars have insisted that the ' suppressed
protasis' before οὐκ ἂν must always be negative—
'else, if it were not so.' But the exception in
' Oed. Tyr.' 220-1,

οὐ γὰρ ἂν μακρὰν
ἴχνευον αὐτός, μὴ οὐκ ἔχων τι σύμβολον,

is apparent only. 'For had I not remained a
stranger, but inquired, I could not have carried the
inquiry far.'

Emphatic negation sometimes takes the form of
oxymoron, i.e. a paradoxical phrase : 'Ajax,' 640 :
ἐκτὸς ὁμιλεῖ, 'He consorts with them outside,' i.e. he
is a stranger to them; 'Phil.' 1153 : ἀνέδην ὅδε
χῶρος ἐρύκεται—'It is defended by abandonment,'
i.e. not defended.

Moods.—In Sophocles the uses of εἰ with subjunctive and of the potential optative appear to be
survivals from an earlier form of speech. In two
places of 'Oed. Col.' 540-1, μή ποτ' . . . ἐπωφέλησα,

1713, μὴ . . . ἔχρῃζες, the traditional reading can
only be defended by supposing an extension of the
idiomatic μὴ ὤφελον by which μὴ with a past tense
is made to express a negative wish. And the
unusual syntax may have been softened to the ear
through phonetic association.

Cases.—Some uses of the genitive and dative
which have been questioned may after all be sound.
'Phil.' 648: ὃ μὴ νεώς γε τῆς ἐμῆς ἔνι, 'Oed. Tyr.' 808:
ὅχου . . . καθίκετο, 'Oed. Tyr.' 198 : τέλει γὰρ εἴ τι
νὺξ ἀφῇ. In Hermann's emendation, τελεῖν, τοῦτο is
awkwardly placed.

An accusative is sometimes left without construction as the sentence proceeds. 'Oed. Col.' 1192:
ἀλλ' αὐτόν—the thread is broken off, and the sense
resumed in 1201: ἀλλ' ἡμῖν εἶκε (sc. τὸν κασίγνητον
μολεῖν).

In *Ibid.* 1649 :

> τὸν ἄνδρα—τὸν μὲν οὐδαμοῦ παρόντ' ἔτι,
> ἄνακτα δ' αὐτόν,

the object of the verb is shifted, and the misleading
phrase corrected in continuing the sentence.

(2) Tragic diction is *condensed.*

In Shakespeare's later manner the energy of the
thought gives rise at once to fulness and compression,
so that the ideas crowd on one another, and make
confusion :

> ' Much like a press of people at a door
> Throng his inventions which shall go before.'

Hence he is often accused of mixed metaphors, as in Hamlet's soliloquy :

'To take arms against a sea of troubles,'

and in 'Macbeth,' I. vii. 12, after the words 'He's here in double trust,' as the sentence proceeds, the additional thought 'And his subject' introduces a fresh duplication. It is needless to multiply illustrations.

In Greek tragedy the same tendency is observable within narrower limits.

In *Similes* the thing compared is spoken of in terms of the comparison. ' Trachiniae ' 116 : βιότου πολύπονον ὥσπερ πέλαγος Κρήσιον ;

Ibid. 130 :

ἀλλ' ἐπὶ πῆμα καὶ χαρὰν (the most probable reading)
πᾶσι κυκλοῦσιν οἷον ἄρκτου στροφάδες κέλευθοι.

In this and other cases (*e.g.* 'Oed. Tyr.' 922-3) the entire sense is only to be obtained by supplying words.

Zeugma.—One verb or adjective is made to serve for two subjects. This mode of speech is too familiar to need illustration. See for instance ' Oed. Tyr.' 1135-6 :

τὸν Κιθαιρῶνος τόπον
ὁ μὲν διπλοῖσι ποιμνίοις, ἐγὼ δ' ἐνὶ
ἐπλησίαζον τῷδε τἀνδρί κ.τ.λ.

Prolepsis.—Two separate points of time are taken by compression into one view, so that by a natural condensation what is really subsequent is

spoken of as if it were simultaneous.   There is a use
of the aorist participle occurring even in prose
narrative in which this irregularity appears.   See
e.g. Herodotus, VII. 106. 1.   Xerxes on his march
appoints Mascames satrap of Doriscus in the place
of Dareius' nominee : κατέλιπε δὲ ἄνδρα τοιόνδε
Μασκάμην γενόμενον κ.τ.λ.   ' This Mascames whom
he left in charge' (not had proved himself but)
' afterwards proved himself a man so meritorious.'
Cp. *Ibid.* 164. 2: τὴν εἰς Μεσσήνην μεταβαλοῦσαν
τὸ οὔνομα.   In ' Oed. Tyr.' 227 : τοὐπίκλημ' ὑπεξελών,
the removal of the offence is the consequence and
not the preliminary of self-exile, but the expression
is condensed.   The most probable reading of ' Oed.
Col.' 547, ἁλοὺς ἐφόνευσα, is an extreme instance of
this use, but is less ridiculous than it has been
represented to be.   It satisfied former editors, who
rendered it by *manifesto occidi*—' I was the murderer
—convicted of the fact.'   The conviction was of
course subsequent to the crime, but the condensed
expression ' trammels up the consequence.'

(3) Tragic diction is *dramatic*, and often needs
to be helped out by action and gesture.   A note of
Capell's on ' King Lear,' V. iii. 265-6, affords a
good illustration of this requirement.

> ' *Kent.*   Is this the promised end ?
> *Edgar.* Or image of that horror ?
> *Alb.*   Fall and cease.'

Capell had been the first of eighteenth-century

critics to point out that 'the "horror" of which the sight was the image is—the horror of the last day, or day of judgment,' and of 'fall and cease,' he says : 'These words were made very intelligible by the action accompanying ; the wide display of his hands, and the lifting up of his eye, both directed towards the heavens, would show plain enough that it is they who are called upon to *fall*, and crush a world that is such a scene of calamity . . . "fall and let things cease ! " ' '

I may add that this view is in keeping with the character of Albany, whose gentle but irresolute nature is unequal to the strain.

'Macbeth,' II. i. 44-5 :

> 'Mine eyes are made the fools o' the other senses
> Or else worth all the rest.'

When these words are simply repeated, without significant gesture, they are unmeaning. While gazing on the fatal vision that 'marshals him the way that he was going,' Macbeth dreamily returns his dirk into the sheath and clutches a second time at 'the air-drawn dagger.' It again eludes his grasp, and thus appears to mock his eyes and make fools of them. But the hallucination regains its power, and as the vision grows in distinctness, he for the moment believes his eyes, although they are contra- dicted by the sense of touch. The actor ought to make this manifest to the spectator.

'Macbeth,' II. ii. 20–31 :

' *Macb.* Hark !
        Who lies i' the second chamber ?
Lady M.   Donalbain.
Macb. (*Looking on his hands*) This is a sorry sight.
Lady M. A foolish thought to say a sorry sight.
Macb. There's one did laugh in's sleep, and one cried " Murder ! "
        That they did wake each other : I stood and heard them ;
        But they did say their prayers, and address'd them
        Again to sleep.
Lady M.   There are two lodg'd together.
Macb. One cried, " God bless us ! " and " Amen " the other :
        As they had seen me with these hangman's hands.
        Listening their fear, I could not say, " Amen,"
        When they did say " God bless us." '

The connection has often been misunderstood.
Lady Macbeth, in her unimaginative way, has her
attention wholly fixed on the actual circumstances.
Macbeth had heard voices in the chamber next to
Duncan's, in which, as she now tells him, Donalbain
was lying ; and when he repeats the conversation,
she explains that Donalbain was not alone. He
had a bedfellow—'there are two lodg'd together.'
It is foolish to suppose that those who waked each
other and cried ' God bless us ! ' and ' Amen ! ' were
' the surfeited grooms.' With appropriate action all
this should be as clear as day.

'Macbeth,' IV. iii. 216 : ' He has no children.'
Macduff turns impatiently from the boy Malcolm,
' yet unknown to woman,' who is trying to comfort
him, and urges Ross to give more details of the cruel
disaster. This meaning was understood by Johnson

and Malone, but recent critics have puzzled over the place, and Brandes pronounces it unintelligible. Right action would place it beyond the reach of doubt.

'Hamlet,' III. i. 89–92:

> 'Nymph, in thy orisons, . . . Well, well, well.'

Ophelia with her prayer-book is walking at the back of the stage. Hamlet has caught sight of her, and for the moment his old passion revives. He apostrophises her in an aside which she does not overhear. To his amazement after what has passed (II. i. 75 ff.) she comes forward and accosts him. He is shocked and his suspicion is aroused. He replies to her as a stranger and a madman. Only thus can the transition be smoothly made from ' Be all my sins remembered ' to ' I humbly thank you, well.' This point is apt to be slurred over when the passage is only read.

Stage directions are less required in Attic tragedy than in Shakespeare, but more than in Corneille or Racine. In the time of the Grand Monarque Electra could not have thrown herself down at the palace gate, nor could Creon have laid hands upon Oedipus. This would have seemed to Voltaire as inexcusable as the buffet in the ' Cid.' In Aeschylus, ' Agamemnon,' 828:

> τὸν δ' ἐπεισφέρειν κακοῦ
> κάκιον ἄλλο πῆμα,

we require the direction 'in saying this Clytemnestra
casts a vicious glance at Cassandra,' and in Sophocles,
'Electra,' 610 : ὁρῶ μένος πνέουσαν, it is obvious
that Clytemnestra shows in some way that she has
been stung to fury. The Chorus, who are in sympathy with Electra, could not speak thus of her.
The words of Jocasta in ' Oed. Tyr.' 746 : ὀκνῶ τοι
πρὸς σ' ἀποσκοποῦσ', ἄναξ, are clearly occasioned
by some gesture on the part of Oedipus.

Persons under stress of emotion do not at once
take in the whole of what has just been said. They
either misapprehend or ask for further information.
What can be more pathetic than the tremulous
' Who ? ' of the deceived patriarch in Genesis xxvii. 33
(A.V.), or in ' Macbeth,' IV. iii. 211 ff., than Macduff's
repeated questions 'My children too?' . . . 'My
wife killed too?' . . . 'Did you say all?' By the
same means the situation is brought more clearly
before the mind of the spectator. So in Sophocles,
'Trachiniae,' when the Messenger has suddenly
poured down his news before her, Deianira asks
(184) :

> τίν' εἶπας, ὦ γεραιέ, τόνδε μοι λόγον ;
> What is this that you have told me ?

The case of ' Oed. Col.' 1250 ff. is not dissimilar.
Interpreters were divided about ἀνδρῶν γε μοῦνος.
Some thought it meant 'weeping alone of men,' as
if men did not often weep in Hellas. Others have
preferred 'unattended by men,' meaning that the

coming of Polynices raised no such apprehension as the approach of Creon, οὐκ ἄνευ πομπῶν (723), had done.   But is Polynices then attended by women?

I suggested in 1872 that Antigone intends to confirm the anticipation of Oedipus in 1171 ff., where he inferred that the Argive stranger who claimed kin with him could be no other than his son.   'Indeed he, and no man else.' This has been censured as 'weak.' I maintain that it is *dramatic*.   The girl in saying this turns to her father and hints what she dares not fully to express.   He in tremulous excitement fails to grasp her meaning, and asks for more explicit information.   She then explains herself and ventures to utter the hated name.

In 'Ajax' 338, ἰὼ παῖ, παῖ, it has been supposed that the hero's first thought on regaining consciousness is to call for his child.   I suggested that the call is for his younger brother, whose presence he sorely needs. This again is waived aside with the remark, 'Tecmessa does not understand him so.' But that is the point of my suggestion.   Ajax, in his helpless misery, longs for Teucer, who alone can support him. Tecmessa, in her maternal solicitude, is terrified to think that 'boy' is meant for Eurysaces. But Ajax impatiently with a loud voice rejoins, 'It is Teucer whom I call!   Where is he?'   If the scene were acted, I believe this would be felt as natural and effective.

The difficulty in 'Oedipus Coloneus' line 1491

would disappear in the performance, if the Chorus
were first to look towards the Acropolis (πατρῷον
ἄστυ γῆς) and then turn their eyes in the direction
of the altar of Poseidon :

> ' Ho ! my prince, come with speed !—or if haply at hand
> On the height where the curved altars stand,' &c.

(4) Tragic diction is *simple* and direct—without
irrelevancies.

How often this truth has escaped interpreters
must be evident to any one who glances over the
pages which Mr. Furniss, in the appendix to his
Variorum edition of ' Romeo and Juliet,' has devoted
to *Runawayes eyes* (' Rom. and Jul.' III. ii. 6).
Juliet is conspiring with Night for a stealthy
purpose, and in imagining chances of discovery
her thoughts turn to those who, like herself, would
avoid detection, such as fugitives from justice or
from hostile pursuit. No one else, she imagines,
is likely to be abroad in the dark, and she prays
that ' runaways' eyes may wink,' *i.e.* not see. This
is subtle, but not recondite. The critics, however,
either suppose the ' runaway' to be Cupid, or the
Night herself ; or would conjecture ' rumour's eyes.'
(Rumour is not Argus-eyed, though ' painted full
of tongues.') In any case they wander from
simplicity.

This rule disposes of some other noted ' emendations.'

In 'Macbeth,' V. iii. 22–3, it was once fashion-able to read with Dr. Johnson :

> 'I have lived long enough : my *May* of life
> Is fallen into the sear, the yellow leaf.'

But an image recalling the gaiety and freshness of youth is out of harmony with Macbeth's present mood. He is weary of the sun ; and the ideas of green foliage and blooming flowers are the last which are likely to occur to him. 'My May of life' is a patch of alien colour, which ruins *chiaroscuro*.

In Hamlet's soliloquy, III. i. 57–8, some have read,

> 'Whether 'tis nobler, in the mind to suffer
> The stings and arrows of outrageous fortune,'

instead of

> 'Whether 'tis nobler in the mind, to suffer
> The slings and arrows of outrageous fortune.'

But the conception of a pitiless shower of various missiles is injured by the introduction of a different idea.

The requirement of simplicity throws doubt also on some ingenious interpretations. It was a sugges-tion of Farmer's that when Hamlet, I. ii. 67, says to Claudius 'I am too much i' the sun,' he intends a play of language between 'sun' and 'son.' This has been accepted and improved upon by recent critics (see Prof. Dowden's note). Such a line of interpretation appears to me misdirected, or at least overdone. The speech is ironical, but the irony is of a much deeper tone. That the assonance or echo of sound may have flitted before the mind of the poet I would not deny, but I cannot think that he deliberately attributed it to Hamlet in this scene.

And the same remark applies with even greater force to the refinements on the preceding line,

'A little more than kin and less than kind.'

Claudius is at once uncle and father-in-law to Hamlet, but there is no love between them. That is all.

In 'Macbeth,' II. iv. 7, 'the travelling lamp' is simpler and therefore better than 'the travailing lamp,' *i.e.* the Sun labouring to overcome the gloom.

In 'Oed. Tyr.' 1222-3, former scholars, including the late Professor E. L. Lushington, were contented to understand, 'To speak truth of thee, thou gavest me to breathe again, and to close mine eyes in slumber.' It is now proposed to introduce an antithesis: 'I owe to thee both restoration and disaster.' But (*a*) in this case, is not $\tau\grave{o}$ δ' $\grave{o}\rho\theta\grave{o}\nu$ $\epsilon\grave{\iota}\pi\epsilon\hat{\iota}\nu$ mere surplusage, out of place in a lyric? And (*b*) though sleep is often put for death, as in 'El.' 509, $M\upsilon\rho\tau\acute{\iota}\lambda os$ $\grave{\epsilon}\kappa o\iota\mu\acute{a}\theta\eta$, to speak at once of disaster as death, and death as sleep, appears to me an affected duplication of imagery, which is unsimple and unworthy of Sophocles. Moreover, the Chorus are lamenting for the fall of Oedipus, and not for disaster to the State, which has been freed from the plague.

'Oed. Col.' 1230–1 :

εὖτ' ἂν τὸ νέον παρῇ
κούφας ἀφροσύνας φέρον,

Schneidewin, was, I believe, the first to take παρῇ as from παρίημι—'when a man has passed the time of careless infancy.' Not to mention that the use of φέρειν is doubtful, and that the plural ἀφροσύνας is not accounted for, it seems to me simpler and more natural to understand, as formerly, ' When youth arrives with her thoughtless follies.'

'Ajax,' 1365 : καὶ γὰρ αὐτὸς ἐνθάδ' ἵξομαι, this is taken to mean, 'For I, too, shall need a grave.' Is not this too sentimental for Ulysses here, who is appealing not to the sympathy but to the common sense of Agamemnon ? And does not the King's rejoinder suit better with the simpler meaning, ' I, too, shall take that course ' (permit the burial) ? 'Ay, every man for his own line.' ' Why not ? '

'Trach.' 554, λυτήριον +λύπημα. Amongst the proposed corrections of the obvious corruption here, that which finds most favour is λυτήριον λώφημα. But is not the natural emphasis on λυτήριον rather weakened by the introduction of a different idea ? I prefer νόημα, which I thought of many years ago, both as simpler, and as naturally resumed in τοῦτ' ἐννοήσασα, infra, l. 578.

(5) Tragic diction is 'sensuous,' *i.e. vivid* not

prosaic. Every word suggests an image, in accordance with the Greek precept, πρὸ ὀμμάτων ποιεῖν.

A Scottish judge, well known for his wit and literary acumen—the late Lord Neaves—once humorously proposed to emend 'As You Like It,' II. i. 14–18, as follows:

> 'And this our life, exempt from public haunt,
> Finds leaves on trees, stones in the running brooks,
> Sermons in books, and God in everything.'

That is hardly a caricature of many proposed emendations of Shakespeare : *e.g.* 'Hamlet,' I. i. 63 :

> 'He smote his leaded poleaxe on the ice.'

In some cases the simple expedient of introducing a dash is needed to prevent a passage being read as prose: *e.g.* in 'Macbeth,' II. ii. 64, ' Making the green—one red.'

In Soph. 'Oed. Tyr.' 44–5, the interpretation suggested by Musgrave, who conjectured ξυμβολάς for ξυμφοράς, approved by Dr. Thomas Young and adopted by Professors Dalzell and Kennedy, ' For I see that conference of counsels *prevails* most among experienced men,' has been rejected on various grounds, but, if for no other reason, would be condemned on account of the prosaic meaning attributed to ζώσας. These critics would be contented to render ζῇ ταῦτα, in Antigone's defence of the unwritten laws ('Ant.' 457), by ' are *in viridi observantia* ' !

I have a similar impression of prosaic flatness

when in 'Oed. Tyr.' 707 ἀφεὶς σεαυτὸν is merely understood to mean 'acquitting yourself.' This legal or judicial use of the word appears to me out of place in poetry. Is it not rather 'casting yourself loose—releasing yourself—from the things you speak of,' i.e. 'letting them go,' 'dismissing them from your thoughts'? Compare 'Ajax,' 484: τάσδε φροντίδας μεθείς.

In 'Oed. Tyr.' 1075-6 the verb ῥηγνύναι has often been taken intransitively, in the sense which properly belongs to the perfect ἐρρωγέναι. It seems to me more 'vivid,' as well as more consonant with usage, to understand it transitively with a personal subject, 'lest she cause evil to break forth'—'let her raise what storms she will!'

In 'Oed. Col.' 1525 'vividness' favours γειτονῶν in preference to γειτόνων. It matters little whether allies are from far or near. But the nearness of the tomb to Athens (Colonus is still a neighbouring township) is important, and the expression brings it vividly to mind.

In Sophocles it sometimes happens that the combination of figurative with condensed expression, and the suggestive use of words having complex associations, give rise to an obscurity which is not easy to remove.

The word καταμᾶν has associations derived from different roots—'to cut off' and 'to gather'—which are combined in the idea of 'reaping.' Hence

when 'the reaper Death' has set his mark upon
Antigone, in consequence of her spreading dust upon
the dead, it is said in highly figurative language
which is not free from confusion that 'the light
which yet shone upon the last fibre of the Laïan tree
is swept off by gory dust sacred to the powers below,
and' (it is added by a 'harsh' zeugma) 'by frenzied
words and a fury-haunted soul.' 'Ant.' 601–3.

In 'Ajax' 159 it is doubted whether πύργου ῥῦμα
signifies 'a tower of defence' or 'means of defending
a tower.' I prefer the former, as more figurative and
more *vivid*.

Are the words in 'Ant.' 1112 to be understood
literally or figuratively? 'I bound (the maiden)
and will be there in person to release (her),' or
figuratively 'It is I who tied the knot and I in person
will unloose it'? I prefer the latter, both as less
prosaic, and as more in agreement with the sequel.
See Chapter X.

(6) Tragic diction is 'passionate'; *i.e. emotional*,
not *frigid*. A phrase which conveys the feeling of
the moment is preferred to one which is correct but
unimpassioned.

Hamlet, in III. i. 67, has been supposed to mean
by 'This mortal coil' the body which hampers and
envelopes the soul; but he is really thinking of the
troublous condition of mortality, as opposed to an
immortal peace.

In 'Macbeth,' V. v. 16, 'She should have died

hereafter,' it has been thought necessary to change 'should' to 'would,' or to understand the passage as if it had been written so; but Macbeth is not weighing probabilities: he is expressing his impatience that the inevitable blow should have fallen *now* when he is beset on all sides with calamities, and not *hereafter* when he might have had leisure to endure it or it might even have come as a relief. The meaning is to be conveyed by placing a strong and passionate emphasis upon 'hereafter.'

In 'Othello,' V. ii. 7, the punctuation suggested by Warburton,

'Put out the light, and then—Put out the light!'

is absolutely required to convey the feeling of the moment.

The words in 'Oed. Tyr.' 1219-20:

δύρομαι γὰρ ὡς περίαλλ' ἰαχέων (or ἰακχίων)
ἐκ στομάτων,

have been variously emended—for example

δύρομαι γὰρ ὥσπερ ἰάλεμον χέων
ἐκ στομάτων.

But is not ἰάλεμον χέων ἐκ στομάτων a somewhat cold expression for lyric verse? And ἐκ στομάτων standing by itself in an emphatic place appears to me otiose and frigid. Some epithet of στομάτων would seem to be concealed by the corruption. I once suggested χαλκέων, comparing χαλκέον ὀξὺ βόω. in Hes. 'Scut. Her.' 243. But is it impossible that

ἰακχίων may have for once a tragic meaning?
The cry of uncontrollable sorrow is compared with
the wild cries of the mystic train.

The use of ὡς still presents some difficulty.
But if περίαλλα is understood as equivalent to a
superlative, the phrase may be compared with ὡς
μέγιστα, ὡς μάλιστα, and the like.

In 'Oed. Col.' 309 : τίς γὰρ ἐσθλὸς οὐχ αὑτῷ
φίλος, Oedipus has been understood to say that,
being a good man, he wishes well to himself as well
as to Athens. That is surely 'frigid.' The true
meaning is given by one of the scholiasts, who
explains φίλος as active. The coming of Theseus
will be fortunate for his own city as well as for the
stranger. His kindness will redound to his own
advantage.

PART II

CHAPTER IX

AESCHYLUS

Chronological order—Choral and epic elements—Miracle play—The
great manner—The *naïveté* of the early stage—Expectation rather
than surprise—Manner of production—Growth of the dramatic
element—Ideal of equity—Religious basis—From chaos to cosmos
—The Orphic movement—Superhuman plays—Meaning of the
'Prometheus'—Development in religious speculation—From the
'Supplices' to the 'Eumenides'—'The Persians,' an historical
drama—Liberty and democracy—Aeschylus and Pindar—Analogy
of Hebrew prophecy—Conclusion.

> I HAVE faith such end shall be:
>   From the first, power was, I knew.
> Life has made clear to me
>   That, strive but for closer view,
> Love were as plain to see.
>
> When see?—When there dawns a day,
>   If not on the homely earth,
> Then yonder, worlds away,
>   Where the strange and new have birth,
> And power comes full in play.—R. BROWNING.

AESCHYLUS, as the servant of Dionysus and votary
of Demeter, is at once dramatist and prophet; and
though it is difficult to distinguish between elements
which are so intimately interfused, it will be convenient to consider separately (1) the form and
(2) the spirit of his extant tragedies.

(1) It is fortunately possible to feel tolerably

certain as to the chronological order, and since the period of the poet's industry was conspicuously one of growth and transition, such an arrangement is more than usually important. In its earliest phase, then, represented by the 'Supplices,' Aeschylean tragedy has more resemblance to a cantata than to a modern drama. The Chorus is still protagonist, and the lyrical portions are far in excess of the dialogue, of which there is only enough to make the action intelligible. The part of Danaus is hardly distinguishable from that of the Coryphaeus; the only other persons are King Pelasgus and the herald of the sons of Aegyptus. All three are shadowy figures, forcibly but crudely drawn.

In the 'Persae' the Chorus again act as protagonist. Atossa and Xerxes, pathetic as they are, have little to say. The most dramatic incident, and this is singularly impressive, is the raising of Darius' ghost. But the main and central impression is given through the Messenger, whose description of the battle of Salamis is epic in form and spirit. The epic factor again prevails in the 'Seven against Thebes,' where, however, the person of Eteocles comes out with great distinctness and force of characterisation. Here for the first time we have a tragic hero massively displayed. Epic breadth on the whole predominates, while the Chorus of Theban women have now a subordinate place.

The 'Prometheus' stands alone among the extant

pieces as a sort of miracle play, but the person of
the Titan evinces an immense advance in dramatic
power. The subject of the Promethean trilogy
will be considered presently. In point of construction there is a harmony and balance of the various
elements, epical, lyrical, and dramatic, not attained
in any of the dramas that have yet been considered.
It is uncertain whether or not by this time the
art of Sophocles had been developed to anything
approaching its maturity, but it seems probable that
the younger poet had in some way reacted on his
great master, and it is certain that in the Orestean
trilogy, Aeschylus had availed himself of his junior
rival's invention of the third actor. It is here that
the dramatic power of Aeschylus attains its highest
realisation. The trilogy is an oratorio, a sacred
drama, and a tragic masterpiece all in one. The epic
breadth remains in splendid narratives such as the
description of the fire signals and the herald's
account of the siege and the storm, but each of these
great passages has its own tone and colour, adapted
to its place in the drama and contributing to the
totality of the effect. Choric song is far extended,
but in the parts of Clytemnestra and Cassandra,
and of Electra in the ' Choephori,' there is a force of
impersonation not hitherto felt. The action of the
' Choephori,' especially towards the close, moves onward with an increasing impetus which marks the
maturity of the drama, while in the ' Eumenides,'

where the main interest again centres in the Chorus, there is a vividness of impersonation which leaves the daughters of Danaus, the Theban women, and even the Oceanides far behind.

It is needless to say that in all seven dramas the 'great manner' is clearly manifest, and the same was doubtless true of the Satyric dramas, of which only a few fragments remain ; the language everywhere retains 'that large utterance of the earlier gods,' bearing some analogy to those parts of Shakespeare where the poet has not found it necessary to subdue his imagination to dramatic exigencies. There is an obvious contrast between the magniloquence of Aeschylus and the subtly smooth elaboration of the Sophoclean style. Such difficulties as are not caused by corruptions of the text are chiefly due to archaic uses, to vernacular idioms, and to boldness and abruptness of metaphor amounting sometimes to a substitution of the symbol for the thing signified.

Neither Aeschylus nor his audience had read the 'Poetics,' and he indulges fearlessly in dramatic foreshortening. In the transcendent action of the 'Prometheus' he takes little or no account of time. In the 'Eumenides,' as is clearly stated, the wanderings of Orestes with the Furies on his track occupy an indefinite period which intervenes between the prologos and the main action, between the Temple of Apollo at Delphi and the shrine of Athena on the Acropolis.

This *naïveté* of the early theatre contributes largely to the grandeur of the main effect. Some recent critics have lost sight of this important truth. They have imagined that the clever Athenian, like the French auditor, loved to exercise his ingenuity by assisting at a mystery to be unveiled, and it has been suggested that the plot of the 'Agamemnon' presupposes an elaborate conspiracy in which Clytemnestra is in collusion with a portion of the Chorus. Her description of the transmission of the news by fire signals, according to this view, is all a barefaced lie, and the beacon on Aegiplanctus is really a token from Aegisthus intimating to Clytemnestra and the conspirators that the ship of Agamemnon has been descried. This theory rests on the presumed impossibility of a fire on Mount Athos being visible from the highest point in Euboea. Now it is a fact that the mountains of Corsica and the Carrara peaks are often seen from the coast of Liguria, at a distance of a hundred miles, and it is commonly said that Elba, a low-lying island, is seen from the heights above Albenga. Surely then it is permissible in poetic fiction to imagine that when a pine forest on the top of Athos had been fired the watchers on Messapius might perceive it. No doubt a further interval is interposed for the storm in the Aegean, the arrival at the coast, and the approach of Agamemnon and his company. But this is sufficiently accounted for by dramatic foreshortening

That the Elders are half-hearted, that they are aware
of something wrong of which the Watchman also
knows, is clear enough, but there is no evidence of
an elaborate conspiracy.

Again, the character of Clytemnestra has been
interpreted as if it could only be explained by
modern psychological analysis, or as if conceived in
the realistic manner of Euripides. That also is to
mar the solidity of the antique. The Queen's main
motive is a mother's revenge overcoming wifely
loyalty and womanly shame. Like Lady Macbeth
she is sickened by the thought of too much blood,
but such compunctious visitings cannot withhold
her from the one great blow, so long and deeply
meditated, so long delayed.

It is dangerous to read between the lines of an
early Greek tragedy. The same misplaced ingenuity
(as I conceive it) supposes Polynices not to have
been at first included amongst the seven Argive
champions, and Eteocles to be *surprised* into his
exclamation : ὦ θεομανές τε καὶ θεῶν μέγα στύγος.
But it is even more true of the earlier tragedy than
of Shakespeare that a characteristic note is ' Expectation in preference to surprise '; see Coleridge's
' Notes on Shakespeare,' p. 64 : ' As the feeling with
which we startle at a shooting star compared to
that of watching the sunrise at the pre-established
moment, such and so low is surprise compared with
expectation.' Simplicity and directness accorded

best with the *naïveté* of the Athenian audience of
the earlier fifth century.

The so-called tragic irony, *i.e.* the contrast
between appearance and reality, is not inconsistent
with the still more tragic ' looking for ' of retribution
or of disaster.   Few things are more pathetic, even
in the book of Job, than the words iii. 25, 26 :

> ' The thing that I greatly feared is come upon me, and that
> which I was afraid of is come unto me.
> ' I was not in safety, neither had I rest, neither was I quiet,
> yet trouble came,'

or in ' King Lear ' than the anticipation of insanity :
' O let me not be mad ! '

The exact manner of the production of an
Aeschylean drama is still a point of great uncertainty.
It may well have been that some arrangement of the
altar of Bacchus served for the place of sanctuary
to which the daughters of Danaus fled ' as doves to
their windows ' ; for the tomb of Darius, or even for
that of Agamemnon.   We do not know when the
scene-painting attributed to Sophocles was introduced ; but it would seem that the house of Pelops,
the temple of Apollo at Delphi and of Athena on
the Acropolis must in some way have been sym-
bolised on the proscenium, and, if so, it stands to
reason that a separate platform, however slightly
raised, assisted the actors in their declamation ; and
in some way the desert rock in the ' Prometheus '

may have been represented there by a special arrangement.

The Aeschylean trilogy as contrasted with the extreme concentration of the first 'Oedipus' approaches the large completeness of Shakespearian tragedy.

Even after the introduction of the third actor, Aeschylus made little use of the innovation, but in place of the multiplicity of single persons, through which the action in Shakespeare is complicated, if not confused, he filled the orchestra and the proscenium with supplementary Choruses which added greatly to spectacular effect. Of the fifty Choreutae supplied by the Choragus twelve formed the Chorus of each play and two or three undertook the leading parts. The remainder were available for the attendants of the daughters of Danaus in the 'Supplices,' for the guards of Aegisthus in the 'Agamemnon,' in the 'Persae' probably for the war-worn and beggared remnant of the host of Xerxes, and for the Areopagites and προπομποί in the 'Eumenides.' [1]

(2) The triumphs of evil destiny are placed by Aeschylus in a distant past, and are contrasted by him with that ideal of equity towards which humanity is guided by beneficent powers. Such, at least, is the teaching of the one trilogy which has remained

[1] Compare Shakespeare, 'The Tempest,' IV. i. 57, 'Bring a corollary': i.e. a παραχορήγημα.

complete—the 'Oresteia'—and such in a more sublime manner was the root conception of the Promethean trilogy, of which only the second drama,
the 'Prometheus Bound,' remains. But the presentation of the evil is not the less impressive for
being contrasted with the good. On the contrary
it is more vividly conceived. That crime which is
the beginning of sorrows extending from generation
to generation, the curse that will not rest till all be
fulfilled, the untameable spirit of revenge, the perilous
consequence of any breach of domestic sanctities,
are delineated with a master hand.

Thus the 'lawless and uncertain thoughts of a
past age were moralised.' The poet felt that the
Marathonian triumph—that 'sun-burst in the storm
of death'—the Salaminian onset, and the Pan-
Hellenic policy of Aristides, gave witness of a spirit
that was not to be overcome of evil, but, as he
believed, was destined to overcome the evil with
good : the spirit of those who nestled under the
aegis of Athena, and listened to the Apolline voices
that preached the higher law. To speak of such an
inspired teacher as one who through the influence
of music found refuge from the miseries of life
amongst the enchantments of art is surely an inadequate view. Something greater than the beautiful
is here : κρεῖσσον' ἢ μορφὴ καλή.

The Marathonian warrior was from first to
last tremendously in earnest in his poetic service

to his countrymen. For the genial Sophocles, as for the gentle Shakespeare, we can imagine times of relaxation, when the deep thoughts that moulded his imaginative creations were veiled with good-humoured tolerance or ironical pleasantry. But in Aeschylus there is a fire which never slumbers, and the tradition which represents him as having been persecuted for his opinions has a strong appearance of truth.

In accordance with what has been said above, his task was to interest and instruct his countrymen through their own legends and their own mythology —much as modern musical composers have based their high-wrought numbers on national dances and on popular airs. But in the half century before his time, what is vaguely known as the Orphic move-ment, due partly to fresh contact with Egypt and the East, had gained much prevalence amongst enlightened Greeks. A new spirit of Pantheism was gradually remoulding Polytheistic Religion, and developing on different lines that side of early specu-lation which had been expressed in such theogonies as Hesiod's. The horror of blood-guiltiness, the sense of human sinfulness and divine wrath, and of the need of purification and atonement, were at the same time greatly deepened. Religious hopes and fears, though still largely turning on ceremonial conditions, became more individual and personal. The movement was widespread, and not confined to those who had been initiated into the Orphic or other mysteries. There is little doubt that it influenced such centres of theosophic teaching as the shrines at Delphi and Eleusis. And Aeschylus, who was not merely a professional artist but an independent teacher, profoundly steeped in all the culture of his time, is not to be too closely identified with the doctrines of any school. It will therefore be more profitable than the detailed discussion of obscure questions, for which the data are defective, to go straightway to the poet himself and to examine the ground ideas of his seven extant tragedies in a brief survey. In speaking of ' ground ideas ' I do not mean that he proceeds deductively from first principles in the construction of his plots, but that in seriously handling a traditional fable he is inevitably guided by the conceptions as to human life at which he has arrived. By taking the seven dramas together with due regard to the order of their production, and considering them in the light of what we can else discern of Hellenic thought in the early fifth century B.C.—with the help also of the fragments of lost plays—we may hope to catch some glimpses of the grave countenance which looks at us from behind the tragic mask, some tones which may be detected amidst the harmonies that thrilled the Athenian auditory.

(1) The morality of Aeschylus, then, is in the first place profoundly religious. He has thought

deeply on the divine attributes and the divine working.

In several of his plays the *dramatis personae* were wholly superhuman. But the only work of this kind which has come down to us is the second or central drama of the Promethean trilogy—the 'Prometheus Bound.' This is not so much a tragedy in the modern sense as a mystery or morality play, embodying symbolically the poet's view of heavenly things.

The 'Prometheus' of Aeschylus has appealed in various ways to the modern imagination. Goethe saw in it the protest of the human intellect against the perversions of Christian theology. To Shelley, the suffering Titan personified the hopes and struggles of the Revolution, prefiguring the destruction of privilege and the triumph of equality and fraternity. To Mrs. Browning he represented all that was noble and beneficent in human progress. But in such 'private interpretations' there is too much of subjectivity. To understand Aeschylus, the trilogy must be taken as a whole. Zeus in the central drama is tyrannical indeed, for in his immature and arbitrary rule he has quarrelled with wisdom and beneficence personified. But the Zeus whom Aeschylus worshipped was of a different mood. For, ages since, the Supreme God and Prometheus had been reconciled; power and wisdom had met together, force and beneficence had kissed each other. This had been brought to pass by the destinies and the law of retribution working in concert towards a consummation in which righteousness should at length prevail.

Not the destruction of an existing order as in Shelley, not the omnipotence of human intellect as in Goethe's lyric, but the ultimate harmonising of apparent opposites in the divine nature, with corresponding peace on earth and good will among mankind, is the ground idea of the trilogy as a whole. In the extant play the opposition culminates and forms indeed an effective protest against any theology in which God is conceived merely as the Almighty, to the exclusion of the other divine attributes of benevolence, equity, and mercy. Zeus as he now reigns—not as he is imagined to have ruled in some distant past—whether as ' winking at the times of ignorance ' or because he had not yet attained perfection—is rather that ineffable power to whom the Chorus of the ' Agamemnon ' appeal :

> ' Zeus—by what name soe'er
> He glories being addressed,
> Even by that holiest name
> I name the highest and best—
> On him I cast my troublous care,
> My only refuge from despair :
> Weighing all else, in him alone I find
> Relief from this vain burden of the mind.
> . . . Zeus, who prepared for men
> The path of wisdom, binding fast
> Learning to suffering. . . .'

But the poet is not to be supposed to have

attained to this conception at a single bound, or to have cleared it from all confusion and ambiguity. In the ' Supplices,' perhaps the earliest of the extant dramas, while the power of Zeus is sublimely expressed, the pleadings of his children or descendants with him are tinged with a pathetic doubtfulness. The poet's faith shone out most brightly towards the end of his career. His thought in its earlier efforts was still struggling within the swaddling bands of tradition and mythology.

Now to descend from the divine into the human sphere. With regard to this there is a corresponding contrast between the former and the latter dispensations ; a corresponding progress from moral Chaos toward moral Cosmos; from wrathfulness to mercy, from revenge to equity, from sheer autocracy to ordered liberty, from a blind fate to righteous retribution ; from divine malignity to divine Nemesis, from the dread Erinyes to the Eumenides who preside over public and domestic peace. Meanwhile the prophecy of Aeschylus, like other great prophetic utterances, is pregnant not only with rich promise for humanity, but with solemn warning. The elemental passions, which he so vividly depicts, are tamed by heavenly influences, but not extinguished. The civilised human being has still a wild trick of his ancestors, and should those latent fires again break forth, then woe be to the world and to mankind. Thus the balance is adjusted.

At first the traditional darkness still hovers over the scene. The appeal of the Danaïdes to Zeus as Io's lover is only temporarily successful, for the sequel, although the drama has perished, is known to have been disastrous. The persecuting cousins in some way vindicate their right, the marriage is solemnised but not consummated, except in the case of Hypermnestra, whose love is won by Lynceus, so that she breaks her rash vow—*splendide mendax*. When taken to task for this, she gives the well-known answer :

> ' Heaven broods with holy longing o'er earth's breast ;
> Earth inly longs for gentle Heaven's embrace ;
> Till showers descending from the brooding Heaven
> Quicken her womb, and she brings forth for mortals
> The grape, the olive, and sustaining corn.
> From that moist marriage, too, the woods are clothed
> With beauty : these are partners of my sin.'

We are reminded of the words of the half chorus at the end of the ' Supplices ' in praise of the gentler mood of Aphrodite.

But the point about the extant play is that it represents a time when the law of sanctuary was not yet absolute, but could still be matter of debate, to be decided only by a popular vote. Indirectly the whole drama is a plea for the claims of natural affection and humanity—for civilised as against barbarous proceeding—and the assertion of a religious sanction for equity and mercy.

The Oedipodean trilogy, of which the extant

part—the ' Seven against Thebes '—appears to have
been the concluding drama, would seem to have
likewise ended in gloom. The tragic Muse still
works beneath the shadow of that elder dispensation
in which the sins of the fathers were visited on the
children, and the dead man's curse lived on to blight
his posterity. Eteocles saves his country, but falls
a victim to a predetermined doom. The main impression is one of pity and terror unrelieved. Yet in
depicting the nobleness of the Cadmean prince's contention against such fearful odds, the poet emphasises
his deep moral conviction that honour and virtue
are of more account than life itself; and in the
description of Amphiaraus, commonly supposed to
contain an allusion to Aristides the Just, an ideal of
disinterested public spirit is held up to view. The
harshness of the situation is further softened by the
sisterly affection of Antigone, who, as afterwards in
Sophocles, defies the edict of the citizens who forbade
the burial of Polynices.

Yet if the poet had ended there, his art might
well have been accused of pessimism. The Erinyes
work only for destruction ; the power of the curse
is absolute ; the sin of Laius is not purged. It
is in the great Orestean trilogy, which has fortunately come down to us almost entire, that the
higher mind of Aeschylus comes clearly forth.
Greek Tragedy is here approaching the stage so
well described by a French critic, quoted in one of

Matthew Arnold's notebooks, as 'the song of
humanity when detaching itself from the gloomy
images of Fate, and setting its face freely towards
the light.' (*Sophocle chanté l'humanité à l'heure où
elle se dégage des fatalités sombres et se dirige libre-
ment vers la lumière.*)

It does not follow that the fatality, which is of
the substance of the legends, is by any means dis-
carded. Fate, Nemesis, and divine anger still form
the warp of tragedy, but the ideas which they
symbolise are modified by the nature of the woof.
Destiny is no longer the blind inexorable power of
primitive belief, but has beneficent aspects, and
works, however slowly, in harmony with eternal
justice. Divine Nemesis is no longer moved by the
mere determination to pull down what is high. It
is only impious self-exaltation that goes before
disaster. The Erinyes are transformed into the
Eumenides, losing nothing of their awful dignity,
but reserving a blessing.

An injustice is done to the poet when the
'Agamemnon' is produced alone; or when, as in the
'Les Erinnyes' of Leconte de Lisle, the action ends
with the catastrophe of the 'Choephori.' That is
to mutilate a grand creation,—as if 'Macbeth' were
ended with the murder of Duncan, or with the
passion of Macduff over the loss of his wife and
children. It would be as reasonable to tell the
story of the Flood without the setting of the bow

in the cloud, or the death of Stephen without his vision of the open Heaven. For it is in the trilogy as a whole that the mind of Aeschylus is fully revealed. The crude morality of a previous generation is corrected ; the ' miserable child's play ' of action and reaction, revenge upon revenge, is finally condemned :

> ' Thanks to the power that wields the sovereign oar
> Resistless, toward the eternal shore.'

The evil-doer must suffer, but this is the work of Him who by a supreme law has made suffering the condition of learning to do well. When right is vindicated, then ' the darkness is past and the true light now shineth ' :

> ' Night is past, behold the day ' : πάρα τὸ φῶς ἰδεῖν.

But the experience of former evil remains to warn mankind of possibilities that may recur, and the heart which exults in this fresh vision of a new ideal has leisure ' to grieve at grievances foregone ' —to make allowance for the embitterment of Clytemnestra, to enter into all the pathos of Cassandra's fate, to fathom the darkness enveloping the house of the Pelopidae, and sympathise with the long agony of Agamemnon's children as they stand before his tomb; to follow Orestes in his wandering, as he slowly expiates his heaven-appointed matricide, and rejoice with him when by the grace of Athena he is once more an Argive and may return to reign in his own country and in his father's home.

The ' Persians ' of Aeschylus is the sole extant example of a Greek historical drama. His prede-cessor Phrynichus had produced a play on the calamity which befell the Ionian name in the sack of Miletus and gave a foretaste of the Persian War. And he had been fined by his countrymen for re-minding them of a personal sorrow. But Aeschylus, only six years after Plataea, was not afraid of present-ing to the Athenians an image of their triumphs in which he himself had shared. The play belongs to an early stage of his career; but he is untrammelled by the time-honoured legends, and his own thought is consequently more clearly apparent.

Dramatic perspective is secured by remoteness of place, which serves instead of remoteness in time. The scene is laid at Susa, the centre of the Persian Empire, at a distance of three months' journey from the Aegean. And for the contrast between the earlier and later dispensations, we have the jubilant antithesis of an ordered liberty to bare autocracy. The Athenians are taught to feel compassion for a fallen foe ; they are warned against the danger of overweening pride, and they are instructed to attri-bute their success, not to man's power or wisdom, but to those free institutions which are the gift to them of Athena. Already the decrees of Destiny are seen to be conditional on human conduct. They may be retarded by wise foresight, or hastened, as in the case of Xerxes, by human folly and sin.

It is observable that while many individual Persians are celebrated, not a single Greek is mentioned by name. Whether this is meant to conciliate jealousies or to emphasise the impression of divine intervention, it gives striking evidence of the feeling of equality which prevailed amongst Athenian citizens, and it may be fairly understood as a Greek equivalent for *Non nobis, Domine*. The spirit of the piece approaches that of our latest war-lyrist:

' The sea-kings loved not boasting, they cursed not him that cursed,
  They honoured all men duly, and him that faced them, first;
  They strove and knew not hatred, they smote and toiled to save,
  They tended whom they vanquished, they praised the fallen brave.' [1]

Yet the praises of Darius imply the possibility of a beneficent paternal monarchy; and the supernatural in tragedy has never been used with more effect than in the apparition of his Ghost. His last words in departing are possibly an echo from the wisdom of some Persian sage. They have something in them of the tone of Omar Khayyam, and of the verse in Ecclesiastes (ix. 10) of which Mr. C. Montefiore says,[2] ' the moral is found in reasonable enjoyment and in fruitful energy. Be active while you can.'

In loftiness of ethical conception the only Greek poet comparable with Aeschylus is Pindar. But

---

[1] *The Sailing of the Long Ships*, by Henry Newbolt.
[2] In his *Bible for Home Reading*.

Aeschylus is by far the more expansive, the more human. Pindar's sympathies are with the scions of great houses, and to them also his warnings and exhortations are addressed. Whether for reproof and admonition or for consolation, the appeal of Aeschylus is to the people at large. Although a brave soldier, he has a pious horror of king-made wars. He sees that popular respect for a throne not established in righteousness is sure to decay, and that freedom itself is valueless without the maintenance of law. And he cares for order in the family no less than in the State. The breach of domestic peace and purity is breach of all It is like the letting out of waters, and must redound to national disaster. Herein Aeschylus is wiser than Plato. And for woman he has everywhere the tenderness that accompanies the truest manhood. His Electra, although embittered, has not the touch of iron which we find in the Electra of Sophocles, and his compassion for the female captives in a conquered city breathes the very spirit of chivalry. The devotion of the Ocean-nymphs who share the fate of Prometheus is measured by the feminine tearfulness of their first approach to him.

Aeschylus has much in common with the Hebrew prophets of the eighth and seventh centuries B.C. Like them he holds before mankind an ideal of righteousness and mercy, of purity and equity. But he differs from them in his bright appreciation of

innocent human joys; and while the glorious city of
the Messianic vision was in the far future, Aeschylus
exulted in a redemption of humanity which he saw
to be actually in progress, and which, among his own
countrymen, he believed to have begun. Though
his latter days were overclouded, and he espied
danger in some threatened innovations, he was
happy in not anticipating the evils consequent on
the Peloponnesian war. Else the end would have
appeared to him as still remote, and he might have
exclaimed with his own Prometheus :

> 'Not so—Not yet. All-consummating Fate
> Ordains this otherwise. When countless woes
> And agonies have bowed me—not before—
> These bonds shall leave me.' [1]

---

[1] The quotations are naturally taken from my own translation
(*Aeschylus in English Verse* : Kegan Paul, 1890). I may also be
permitted to refer to my volume on *Religion in Greek Literature*
(Longmans, 1896), and to *A Guide to Greek Tragedy* (Rivingtons).

CHAPTER X

SOPHOCLES

Characteristics—Disillusionment—Yet unclouded faith—' Human
nature '—' The noble living and the noble dead '—The unwritten
law—Revenge as a motive, how far modified—Contrasts of
character—Subordinate persons—The curse of Oedipus—Action
through narrative—Supposed flaw in the ' Antigone '—' The irony
of Sophocles '—Last plays—Comparison with Shakespeare—
Love of Nature—The pathetic fallacy.

> Perchance his dying gaze, so satisfied,
> Was lightened, and he saw how vast a scope
> Ennobled them of power to dare beyond
> Their mortal frailty in immortal deeds,
> Exceeding their brief days in excellence,
> Not with the easy victory of gods
> Triumphant, but in suffering more divine ;
> Since that which drives them to unnumbered woes,
> Their burning deep unquenchable desire,
> Shall be their glory, and shall forge at last
> From fiery pangs their everlasting peace.
>> From *The Death of Adam*, by LAURENCE BINYON.

IN Sophocles the form and spirit of tragedy have
coalesced into a perfect whole. When one of his
dramas is compared with one of Aeschylus or with
the remaining trilogy the most apparent difference
is an increase of concentration; and this characteristic attains its highest development in the first

'Oedipus.' The antecedent circumstances, which in the 'Antigone' and the 'Ajax' are somewhat fully set forth at the opening, are here reserved for the pause of awe-stricken suspense which precedes the crisis, and the sequel, which in those two dramas is in a manner separated from the principal action—the last exit of Antigone and the death of 'Ajax' making a perceptible break—in the 'Oedipus Tyrannus' follows almost continuously, while the protagonist still holds the scene. This last remark is likewise true of the 'Electra.' In the 'Trachiniae' the severity of concentration is in so far relaxed as the death of Deianira and the entrance of Heracles may be said to shift the centre of gravity, making a polarity of interest which the mediating personality of Hyllus binds in unity. In the two remaining plays, belonging to a later time, the form is further altered, and the action instead of moving onward towards a fatal catastrophe passes through a succession of obstacles to a desired end.

It cannot be assumed that this course of evolution corresponds to what is said to have been Sophocles' own account of his dramatic career, as 'having first played for a while with Aeschylean bombast, then attained to greater precision and concinnity, until finally it rested in that ethical manner which he felt to be the best.' But it is certainly true that in the 'Philoctetes' there is a depth of psychological insight, and in the second

' Oedipus ' a mellowness of spiritual tone, which we should in vain look for elsewhere.   The earliest of the extant dramas were long subsequent to the death of Aeschylus ; yet in the ' Antigone ' and the ' Ajax ' as compared with the first ' Oedipus ' it is not altogether fanciful to discern some reminiscence of the Aeschylean trilogy.   All seven plays, however, belong to the poet's maturity, between the fifth and the last decade of the fifth century B.C., and are all pervaded by a common spirit.

Sophocles had accepted from his predecessor the tradition that tragic drama makes for domestic purity, for equity and mercy, for protection to the suppliant and the injured stranger, for moderation in resentment, and the glorification of all that is noblest in humanity.   Less bold in speculation than Aeschylus had been, he still strongly sympathised with the mystical worship of Dionysus and Demeter and revered the gods of the unseen world.   His Athenian patriotism is consistent with a strain of feeling that is individual and lies at the root of family life.   He shares deeply in ' that primal sympathy which having been must ever be,' that vein of natural affection which looks beyond the grave, and is the source of a heroism not of this world.

On the surface of his dramas there is certainly a tone of disillusionment.   He cannot be said, like Aeschylus, to have his ideal in the present. \ The eternity of justice and of the unwritten law is   Soph₁

maintained in the face of facts which seem to contra-
dict them, or at least to delay their fulfilment.| The
idea of fate in Sophocles is an equivalent for the
unaccountable element in human experience,[1] 'the
burden of the mystery of all this unintelligible
world.' For him the evil to be contended with is
not in the far distant past, but in the actual present.
That does not lead the poet to abate one jot of
heart or hope; he holds fast by the strong faith
that the noble spirit, if overclouded for awhile by
his own errors, conscious or unconscious, through
the wrong-doing of others, or the inheritance of a
burdened life, will in the end be vindicated and
accepted of Heaven.

Thucydides presents his history as a record of
facts which actually occurred, and the like of which
in accordance with the tendencies of 'human
nature' must often occur hereafter. That statement is the first appearance in literature of the
generalised conception of human nature regarded as
a concrete whole. Thucydides and Sophocles were
contemporaries, and the same reality which the
historian formulated was no less steadily, if more
ideally, contemplated by the poet of the Periclean
age. His glance had not, and could not have, the
vast range and comprehensiveness of Shakespeare's,
that was enriched by the experience and reflection

---

[1] See Machiavelli's *Prince*, ch. xxv., on Fortune and Free Will
(pp. 167, 168 of Mr. Ninian Thomson's translation. Kegan Paul, 1882).

of another two thousand years. In the sixteenth century, the nature of mankind was far less simple, the conditions far more complex, the inheritance of thought concerning it infinitely more full and varied. Yet in the grasp which either poet had upon the facts of life, how much there is in common! They are akin even in their limitations. Both lived amidst the environment of an aristocratic society, and could not escape from the influence of its traditions. The Athenian's interest at least was centred on

> ' The great society alone on earth,
> The noble living and the noble dead.'

Antigone's act of self-devotion is supported not only by religious conviction, but by the pride of race. In defying the authority of Creon, she not only condemns the impiety of his edict, but despises him as an overbearing upstart. As she is led off to her death, she appeals to her Cadmean ancestry,[1] whose sacred images adorned the palace, to look down and witness by what mean instruments she is oppressed for reverencing the dues of piety.

There is hardly any trace in Sophocles of that large sympathetic interest in the people as such which is so marked a feature in Aeschylus. Yet the poet's ideal of true nobility is not merely conventional. The kings of Sparta and Mycenae make

---

[1] This I take to be the meaning of Θήβης οἱ κοιρανίδαι (940), which hardly suits with her address to the πόλεως πολυκτήμονες ἄνδρες (841).

a poor figure in the 'Ajax' beside the bastard brother and the captive bride.

'The noble spirit,' whether in man or woman, comes near indeed to express the Sophoclean ideal. The trials and disasters to which that spirit is liable form his constant theme ; the essential nobleness of Ajax, Oedipus, Philoctetes, Antigone, Electra, Deianira, is finally vindicated, and their persons are accepted by the supreme powers—it may be in life, it may be after death. Every spectator must have felt that it is better to die with Antigone than to live with Creon.

In Sophoclean tragedy, attention is always fixed on an individual destiny. The fable is taken for granted. It was familiar to the audience and had been treated before, if not in drama, yet in passages of epic and lyric poetry which were generally known. That which really matters is the poet's treatment of the fable, his conception of the principal personalities, and the religious and ethical ideas on which the action turns.

The orator Lysias, in his speech for the prosecution of Andocides, quoted Pericles as having spoken to the following effect :

'In dealing with impiety not only written laws are to be observed, but account must be taken also of those unwritten principles of law on which the Eumolpidae base their decisions. These no authority may abrogate nor contravene; and no man knows from whom they came. The recompense for their violation rests not with men but with the gods.' That is a prose version of the immortal lines in which Antigone defends her disobedience to the edict of Creon. And the testimony of Lysias is corroborated by a similar expression in the famous funeral oration which Thucydides attributes to the Athenian statesman (Thuc. ii. 37).

It follows that the idea of the eternal laws, so magnificently celebrated in the second stasimon of the first ' Oedipus,' had already found a place in Eleusinian tradition. For the Eumolpidae were the exponents of the religion of Demeter.

That idea is deeply inherent in the Periclean poet's ' criticism of life.' He is no longer, like his predecessor, engaged in contrasting a shadowy past with a glorious present, that is pregnant with still greater glory in the near future. The present may be dark, the future doubtful : but for present, past, and future equally the same principle of divine justice holds, has held, and shall for ever hold. In spite of human error, in spite of suffering and disaster, the pure in heart is justified, the wrong-doer is condemned. This truth is felt throughout, even when not asserted in so many words. ' God works in a mysterious way ' : but the poet's faith does not falter. He has sounded the abyss of human evil and of mortal misery ; but ever and anon he turns his gaze towards the serene and cloudless empyrean,

wherein reigns from everlasting the ageless, unattainted majesty of the moral ideal.

The conception of Sophocles does indeed come
short in one respect of the highest known to Shakespeare. The Christian forgiveness of enemies is not
yet realised, even in thought. That hostility should
not be carried beyond the grave; that the noble
heart may be moved with pity for a fallen foeman;
that enmities, between kinsmen at least, may, for
aught we know, be atoned amongst the dead; that
Zeus has mercy for his counsellor, that natural
affection ought to prevail over unkindness, are reflections tending to heal an else incurable wound.
But even in the plays of reconcilement there is
something still unreconciled. The curses of Ajax
and of Oedipus, the vindictiveness of Electra, are
utterly unrelieved with any tinge of gentleness.
When Antigone prays that her cruel enemies may
suffer 'no worse than they inflict,' that is only
because worse is not imaginable. The rage of
Heracles against his faithful wife is silenced, but
only by the revelation of his own impending doom.
Plato's thought that the just man will not harm an
enemy is in advance of Sophocles. But in another
way the philosopher, in aiming higher, descends
below the standard of the tragic poet. Those
domestic sanctities which Plato desired to abrogate
for his philosopher-kings are for Sophocles as for
Aeschylus the divinest of bonds.

To describe the higher law which Sophocles up-
holds as merely a law of moderation, is an inadequate
judgment. He sees life steadily—that is true—but
with an earnestness of fervid sympathy that is not
the less intense for being subdued. The volcanic
fires of Aeschylus are in him transmuted into a clear
and smokeless flame.

In the endeavour to represent and estimate the
sadness of life, one does not look in ancient poetry
for the inwardness and reflective depth of Shakespeare. The tragedy of a heart divided against
itself, the

> 'limèd soul, that struggling to be free
> Is more engaged,'

the double nature of Macbeth, the alternating blasts
of affection and bitterness, of love and jealousy, are
complications which belong to the self-consciousness
of the modern world; and yet the conflict in the
mind of Neoptolemus, between friendship and ambition, is presented with the finest psychological
insight—and it may be remarked in passing that
there are kindred modern touches in Euripides.

One feature in which Sophocles is excelled by
Shakespeare alone is the subtle treatment of con-
trasted personalities, and their mutual interaction.
It is enough to name Antigone and Creon, Ajax and
Tecmessa, Oedipus and Tiresias, Deianira and Iole,
Theseus and the elders of Colonus. Especially, as I
have elsewhere observed, Sophocles and Shakespeare

alike throw into prominence the passionate nature of
the tragic hero by placing beside him the man who
is not passion's slave—Odysseus, Theseus, Banquo,
Horatio, Kent. In producing this effect, the poet
was of course assisted by his own invention of the
third actor. It has even been thought that in one
passage of the second 'Oedipus' four speakers were
together present on the stage. To go beyond this
point would not have been according to the spirit of
the ancient drama. Messengers and other insignifi-
cant persons, even slaves and shepherds, have often
an important part in the action; and it should
be remembered that the figures grouped on the
proscenium were not confined to those who spoke;
there were companions, attendants, guards and
others to add completeness and verisimilitude to
the scene. Creon in the 'Antigone,' at least on his
second entrance, is not unaccompanied. In the
'Ajax,' besides the silent person of the child, there
is the slave who leads him; and Teucer has several
assistants in preparing for the hero's burial at the
close. The suppliants of various ages at the opening
of the first 'Oedipus' form a special group. In the
'Electra' there is the silent person of Pylades; in
the 'Trachiniae' there is Iole with the other captives, the bearers of Heracles, and the maidens whom
the Chorus invite to accompany them in following
the hero to his pyre. The disguised mariner in the
'Philoctetes' has a comrade with him, and in the

second 'Oedipus,' Theseus, at least on his return from the rescue, is attended by his men.

The supplementary dialogue filling up the interstices of the action, which in Shakespeare is contributed by 'first and second lords, first and second gentlemen,' &c., is much more aptly furnished by the Chorus of a Greek play, either as a whole or in sections, or as represented by their leader. And yet those side-lights by which Shakespeare indicates the relation of a tragic action to the world at large, or its effect on a wider public (as in 'Macbeth'), are occasionally anticipated by Sophocles even in the dialogue; as when Haemon in the 'Antigone' reports to his father the murmurs in the city, or when the Messenger in the 'Ajax' describes the threatened attack of the Achaeans on Teucer, or when the rude busybody pictures Lichas as haranguing the Trachinian mob.

Of the Sophoclean hero and heroine something has been already said in the chapter on tragic persons; but it is a point deserving special remark, that the most genial of men should have repeatedly chosen to illustrate the effect of continued suffering on an impassioned nature in producing a fixed and dominant idea. Electra and Philoctetes are striking instances of this. And the same observation applies to the obdurate resentment of Oedipus against his sons. The final curse on Polynices is the renewal of an earlier imprecation. The scholiast, Brunck, and Hermann agree in referring the words to the incident in the old legend, which was familiarly known to everyone who saw the play. Schneidewin and Sir Richard Jebb believe the aged king to be merely repeating what he had lately said to Ismene. The latter critic accuses those who hold the earlier view of derogating from the dramatic art of Sophocles. But the indignant outburst against his sons, which was prompted by the report of Ismene, was not formal or full enough to take the place of those personified curses so impressively described by Aeschylus in the ' Seven against Thebes,' and no doubt narrated in a preceding passage of the same trilogy;—which, as a father's Erinyes, pursued Eteocles and Polynices to their doom. In this and in much else Sophocles follows closely in the footsteps of an epic tradition that was matter of common knowledge to his audience.

It has often been observed that Sophocles produces many of his tragic effects through narrative. But the action is, notwithstanding, steadily progressive; and regularity of climax is observed both in regard to the whole and to the several parts, as for example in the speech of Hyllus, describing his father's agony. (It may be noticed, by the way, that the large proportion of space occupied by such narrative speeches in the ' Trachiniae ' is partly due to the isolated position of the heroine.)

The speech of the Second Messenger in the

'Antigone' is another notable example of the same thing. Many readers of the play have been struck by the apparent strangeness of the conduct of Creon, who, when advised to release the maiden and to bury the prince, proceeds first to the burial of Polynices. Professor Jebb pronounces this to be a flaw in the construction of the piece, and accounts for it as intended to provide for a rhetorical climax; but surely the climax thus obtained is not merely rhetorical. If Creon had acted otherwise, Antigone would have been released, and the tragic effect would have been incomplete. The solution of the apparent difficulty turns upon the poet's conception of the character of Creon. His resolution is broken down by the prophecy of Tiresias, which affects him, however, not with pity or remorse, but with superstitious terror. He is not solicitous for the life of Antigone, nor for the consequences to Haemon, of which he has not the faintest conception, but for the divine retribution which is threatening the State. On that all his cares are fixed. He seeks, by performing the religious rite which he had impiously forbidden, to avert the anger of the gods. It is only afterwards, through the deaths of Haemon and Eurydice and their curses falling upon his head, that the natural affection, so long suppressed, recoils in a fearful Nemesis.

For the contrast of situations—present and future, apparent and real—'tragic irony' is a term which

in our language seems to be firmly established in
common use. In the first volume of my edition of
Sophocles, published in 1872, I endeavoured to show
that, as characterising the dramatic art of Sophocles,
this expression is apt to be misleading:

'It detracts from the simplicity and tenderness
which are amongst the chief merits of the Sophoclean drama. It injures the profound pathos of
Greek tragedy by suggesting the suspicion of an
arrière pensée, of the poet's face behind the mask,
surveying his own creations with a sardonic smile.
It puts in the place of the Athenian spectator,
with his boundless susceptibility of emotion, an
imaginary reader or student, who has leisure to reflect on matters external to the immediate action,
and abundant calmness of judgment to give a dis-
passionate verdict in the controversy between God
and man.'

It is vain to deprecate an accepted mode of
speech—as vain as to object (see above, p. 77) to
the common English uses of the words ' climax ' and
' catastrophe.' But it is essential to plead that the
term ' irony ' in this connection should be stripped
of some associations which ordinarily cleave to it ;
such as the smile of conscious superiority, the dissembled laugh, the secret mockery of the unfortunate
—everything in short which impairs the fulness of
emotional sympathy.

If by irony is meant *pathetic contrast*, then

Sophoclean irony is subtle in the extreme. The poet employs it, be it remembered, not to hide from the spectators a mystery that is presently to be unveiled, but rather to excite their expectation, and to move their awe and pity as they perceive the unconsciousness of the agents as to the event. The solemn curse on the unknown malefactor in the mouth of Oedipus, so worded as to recoil in every particular upon himself; the entrance of Jocasta, intended to reassure him, but in the sequel awakening his despair; these and other notes of the great tragic masterpiece are capital instances of what is meant. Such means belong to the general stock-in-trade of the tragic poet. In the essay above quoted I have adduced several similar touches from Shakespeare. ('Cymb.' Act II. sc. iii. l. 152; 'Jul. Caes.' I. ii. 19–21; I. ii. 313; 'Macb.' I. iv. 11–14; 'Oth.' III. iv. 30–32.) I might have added 'Richard II.' I. i. 116–117, where Richard says of Bolingbroke,

> 'Were he my brother, nay, my kingdom's heir,
>   As he is but my father's brother's son,'

and 'Macbeth,' II. iii. 25, where Macduff, the destined avenger, enters unconsciously on the scene of Duncan's murder; besides, of course, Othello's 'honest Iago.'

The dark tradition of a malignant destiny, inherent in the tragic fable, is tempered, even in Aeschylus, with compassion for the unthinking victim. 'God laughs at the excited mortal,' and

' has him in derision.' Yes, but when the Athenian audience witness it, there is pity mingled with their awe. That is still more true of the Sophoclean hero, whose unconsciousness of coming fate is accentuated by many subtle turns of language, and a still stronger compassion is awakened when the unconsciousness is exchanged for a fearful anticipation of disaster, as when Deianira discovers the nature of the supposed love-charm, or when Polynices goes forth to rejoin his army after realising the significance of his father's curse. Once more, as a tragic motive, ' expectation is more effective than surprise.'

The analogy which Mr. Churton Collins and others have pointed out between the latest phase of Shakespeare and ' the two dramas with which Sophocles took his leave of life,' the ' Philoctetes ' and the ' Oedipus Coloneus,' is in my opinion real and instructive. ' All have the same burden—purification by suffering, symbolic revelation of the just and merciful wisdom of that inscrutable power to whom man's most fitting tribute is submission and patience.' Sir Richard Jebb objects that if the external evidence were different, what now are thought to be symptoms of advancing age might have been construed as indicating the immaturity and sanguine temper of youth. It is of course possible that Sophocles may have concluded some of his earlier plays as Aeschylus had done, with a desired event. The ' Ajax ' ends with a partial reconciliation. Nor

is it necessary to suppose that all the poet's later
productions resembled the two which happen to remain. But such considerations cannot remove the
impression which a contemplation of the series of
the seven extant dramas is fitted to produce. The
obvious relaxation of tragic intensity, the mellowness
and ethical mildness of the whole effect in the second
' Oedipus' and the 'Philoctetes' suggest a manifest
parallel to the altered tone of Shakespeare when he
had passed the meridian of his career. Milford
Haven, Bohemia, and the desert island have not a
merely fanciful correspondence to Colonus and the
Lemnian shore. Shakespeare was not old, but he
had retired from active work, and may well be supposed in a relative sense to have felt some approach
of old age. It would seem also that the dramatic
taste of the contemporary audience was altering, so
as to prefer romance and melodrama to purely
tragic themes ; and something of the same kind had
happened to the Athenian Theatre when Euripides
produced the ' Orestes' and the ' Andromeda.'

A few words may be added with regard to those
passages in which Sophocles incidentally anticipates
the modern feeling for Nature. The praises of
Colonus in the second ' Oedipus' have often been
quoted in this connection, but the charms there
described are those of a well-cultivated and richly
irrigated garden-ground, an asylum for song-birds,
with dense foliage, bright fruitage, ever-blooming

flowers, revered for its sacred associations, the object
at once of worship, love, and pride. The tone of the
ode is in keeping with the solemn peacefulness of
the theme. Of a different order are the allusions to
natural scenery in the other plays, *e.g.* Antigone's
appeal to Dirce and the sacred fields of Thebes; the
apostrophe of Ajax to the wooded headlands of the
Troad, and his farewell to the plain itself, with its
rivers and streams; or the apostrophe to Cithaeron
in the first 'Oedipus,' reminding one of 'the sleep
that is among the lonely hills.' Other picturesque
touches are the address to snow-smitten Cyllene as
the abode of Pan, the allusion to the same mountain
and to Helicon as the haunts of Hermes, and the
wanderings of Eros amongst rustic homes; or once
more the imagination of the Theban elders that the
forbidden criminal is hiding in lonely exile amongst
rocks and caves. But the nearest approach to what
has been called the pathetic fallacy is made in the
'Philoctetes,' where the natural environment of the
hero on his desert rock is indicated with especial
insistence. Repulsed by all human associates, his
naturally affectionate heart has wound itself about
the stern and rude concomitants of that houseless
home :

> ' Oh ye, my comrades in this wilderness,
> Rude creatures of the rocks, oh promontories,
> Creeks, precipices of the hills, to you
> And your familiar presence I complain,
> Of this foul trespass of Achilles' son.'

Even when at last persuaded to return, he casts a lingering look behind :

> ' Ye nymphs of meadows where soft waters flow,
> Thou ocean headland, pealing thy deep knell,
> Where oft within my cavern as I lay
> My hair was moist with dashing south wind's spray,
> And ofttimes came from Hermes' foreland high
> Sad replication of my storm-vexed cry ;
> Ye fountains, and thou Lycian water sweet—
> I never thought to leave you, yet my feet
> Are turning from your paths—we part for aye.
> Farewell! and waft me kindly on my way,
> Oh Lemnian earth enclosed by circling seas.' [1]

There is a similar feeling for the charms of natural environment in the allusions to his Melian home.

---

[1] The quotations are from my translation of *Sophocles* : ' The Seven Plays in English Verse ' (J. Murray).

CHAPTER XI

THE GROWTH OF SERIOUSNESS IN SHAKESPEARE

Period of apprenticeship—Closing of London theatres—Poems—The
heart of Shakespeare—' Romeo and Juliet '—Tragic element in the
higher comedy—Chronicle plays—Deepening of the tragic note
in the last days of Elizabeth—The Roman plays—' Antony and
Cleopatra '—Notes.

The utmost that any one student can hope to achieve in the
study of a genius such as Shakespeare's is to draw nearer to it from
those points of view which are open to him—not indeed disregarding,
or rashly undervaluing, the significance of the rest, but satisfied with
the certainty that even to the swiftest perception and to the most
conscientious research many veins of treasure must remain closed. . . .
But every true student labouring in his province will add to the progress of a work which weakness alone would abandon on the pretext
of its seeming interminable.—DR. A. W. WARD.

IT is certain that already at the age of thirty Shake-
speare could on occasion be 'deep contemplative.'
The stanzas quoted in a former chapter from
'Lucrece' (published 1594) are sufficient evidence of
that. It is therefore unnecessary to suppose, with
Mr. Wyndham, that the more reflective passages in
'Love's Labour's Lost,' 'The Comedy of Errors,' or
' Henry VI.' were afterthoughts added in some later
revision. The development of this serious vein in
him may be traced through several stages, marked

by events both public and private which may be
assumed to have affected him : (1) the closing of the
London theatres on account of the plague in 1593 ; [1]
(2) the troubles towards the end of Elizabeth's reign
—the clouds that gathered round her setting (1601) ;
and (3) lastly the poet's establishment in New Place
and his retirement to his native Stratford about 1607.

The first period, ending with 1592, is that of his
theatrical apprenticeship, under the combined influences of Greene, Peele, Kyd, and, above all, Chris-
topher Marlowe.   There is strong evidence of his
having had a part in the dramas of the Contention
and the tragedy of 'The Duke of York,' as well as
in the revision of these dramas which took shape in
the three parts of 'Henry VI.'   And it is probable
that he also had to recast the tragedy of 'Titus
Andronicus'—that the fable and the original plot
were of his choice or invention can hardly be
believed.   In some passages, at least, of the third
part of 'Henry VI.' Shakespeare's hand may be
recognised beyond a doubt, especially in Queen
Margaret's speech at Tewkesbury, Act V. sc. iv.
That at this time he was profoundly influenced by
Marlowe and also by Kyd is manifest, and before
escaping altogether from his servitude to the Tragedy
of Horrors, we find him stamping with supreme
dramatic genius his own continuation of the histories

See Wyndham's *Poems of Shakespeare*, p. 217 ; note on *Venus
and Adonis*, lines 508-9-10.

in 'Richard III.' Not only Richard himself, but
Clarence, Hastings, Elizabeth, Margaret, and the
subtle Buckingham—whose subtilty {is no match
for Gloster's—rise up before us with all the attributes of real humanity. The scene, after Margaret's
return from France, in which she comes forward as
an avenging fury, is unsurpassed in its combination of rhetorical with dramatic power. But the
presentation of Richard himself has not yet the
depth, complexity, and convincingness of a Shakespearian tragic hero of the first rank. The poet is
not contented with conveying to us the attributes of
the royal villain through his acts, or allowing these
to explain their motives. His magnificent description of himself at the opening of the play, and the
contrast which he draws between his character and
that of Clarence, read like a glorified version of some
morality play; and his sudden remorse at the last,
which may be compared with that of Marlowe's
Dr. Faustus, has too little relation with what precedes to be quite believable : it has not been prepared
for, like the despair of Macbeth. The very qualities
which delighted the contemporary audience, and have
still an irresistible charm for the average spectator,
belong to the immaturity alike of the artist and of
his public.

If, as there is some reason to think, Shakespeare
had previously contributed to the play of 'Edward
III.,' he had found there a task, and had been yoked

with a fellow-artist, more congenial to his own original vein.

There is much truth in the remarks of Halliwell-Phillipps upon this subject : 'If it is thought probable that Shakespeare's career of imitation expired with his treading in some of the footsteps of Marlowe, and that he had not, at the latest time when ' Edward III.' could have appeared, achieved a popularity sufficient to attract imitators of his own style, then there will be at least an excusable surmise that his work is to be traced in parts of that historical drama. Every now and then one meets with it in passages, especially in the scenes referring to the King's infatuation for the Countess of Salisbury, which are so infinitely superior to the rest of the play, and so exactly in Shakespeare's manner, that this presumption under the above-named premises can scarcely be avoided.'

The poet's emancipation seems to have been completed when, after the closing of the theatres, he sought and found a patron in Lord Southampton. It is not unreasonable to conjecture that it was during the enforced leisure which gave time for the poems, that he ceased to be an imitator and discovered his own native, untaught, and Heaven-inspired vein. While again submitting to the shackles of contemporary fashion, the poet's heart and mind now revealed themselves in their true colours. In the dedication of ' Venus and Adonis,' ' the first heir of his invention,' he vows to take advantage of all idle hours, till he have honoured his patron with some *graver* labour. The subject of 'Venus and Adonis' is one on which the wits of the time had lavished much licentious verse, and Shakespeare, as he well knew how, has of course treated it appropriately.   There is a certain warmth of colouring as in a painting of Titian, with a dash of Rubens thrown in.   The heathen goddess is not an Imogen or a Miranda.   But what an ideal light suffuses the whole picture, and what a large humanity!   What a world of unwholesome phantasy is chased away before this impulse from a Warwickshire vernal wood!   Nothing in English literature to be compared with it had appeared since Chaucer. In the description of the hare hunt, with which the goddess tries to detain her unwilling captive, the heart of the Stratford poet, from which nothing was alien that was natural, is revealed in all its tenderness. And if the opening part is censured as luxurious, it is balanced by the picture of a divine sorrow—lightly touched, of course, in accordance with the romantic scheme.   In the long poem which followed this, the 'graver labour,' also a favourite subject of Renaissance verse, the narrative (in the manner of the time) is overladen with reflections on the situation, but, as we have seen, the reflections are such as argue a mind bent on contemplating the depth of human things.

In 'Richard II.' the heart and mind thus dis-

closed find their full and unrestricted outlet: the
Marlowesque bombast has departed and the gentle
muse of Shakespeare is unveiled—even the verse is
subdued to an elegiac tone. For sheer poetic quality
this stands alone amongst the history plays, and
of the English histories there is none which more
deserves the epithet of tragic, although the tragedy
is of the milder type and is less venturous than what
was afterwards attempted and achieved. The character of Richard, 'that sweet lovely rose,' with all
its glaring weakness and inconsistency, is familiar
to all, and it is needless to remark with what skill
the poet has contrived to enlist the sympathy of
the audience for the fantastic and *fainéant* king,
and to retain it to the last, when the spirit of
the Plantagenet, though overgrown with follies and
deluded with idle fancies, breaks forth in the one
spasmodic act of self-defence which precedes his
murder. Nor can anything be more characteristic
of the poet than the visit of the groom and his
description of the behaviour of 'roan Barbary.'

In 'Romeo and Juliet,' Shakespeare's first great
tragedy, while poetic expansiveness still strives with
dramatic concentration, the mastery of form is even
more conspicuous than in 'Richard III.' The poet
has already hit upon the normal tragic movement
which I have attempted to delineate in Chapter VI.
The change of fortune coincides with the termination
of Act III., and Act IV. sustains the interest through

the development of the sequel, leading directly to the
catastrophe, while the piece is duly rounded off with
the speech of the Prince. 'Romeo and Juliet'
remains the everlasting record of the sweetness and
the sadness attendant upon true love in youth :

> 'Making it momentary as a sound,
> Swift as a shadow, short as any dream ;
> Brief as the lightning in the collied night,
> That in a spleen unfolds both Heaven and earth—
> And ere a man hath power to say Behold !
> The jaws of darkness do devour it up.'

But if the poet had ended there, he would not
have earned the commendation of Johnson :

'Love is only one of many passions, and as it
has no great influence upon the sum of life it has
little operation in the dramas of a poet who caught
his ideas from the living world, and exhibited only
what he saw before him. He knew that any other
passion, as it was irregular and exorbitant, was a
cause of happiness or calamity.' The tragic handling
of deeper, more complex and far-reaching emotions
was reserved for a later stage, when his muse had
'summed her pens' and he had attained that mastery
of human nature, and of the facts of life, which has
given him his unrivalled supremacy.

Throughout the histories and comedies of the
middle period there is a strain of exuberant vitality
and prevailing joyousness which culminates in the
person of Prince Hal and the triumphs of the patriot
king. Yet in the passages which precede the death

of Arthur, in the presentiment of Hotspur (1 'Hen. IV.,' V. ii. 98), and in the heroic scenes at Agincourt more than one tragic note is struck; and in 'The Merchant of Venice' both Antonio and Shylock are all but tragic persons—only not quite so because of the fantastic situation, which it is impossible to take quite seriously—the pound of flesh. But the contrasted pictures of the friend and enemy had in them elements akin to tragic feeling. The poet seems to have been drawn aside from his first intention of giving the part of protagonist to the title-rôle, and making Antonio in reality, as well as in name, the hero of the play, by the fascinating ugliness of the part of Shylock. And thus a drama which should have had for its theme the beauty of friendship, passing the love of women, is familiarly known to us by its lifelike exhibition of the passion of ruthless malignity. Antonio's devoted friendship for Bassanio—which draws from the light-minded Magnifico the fine remark

'I think he only loves the world for him,'

and is so nobly appreciated by Portia—nowhere comes out with such vividness or intensity as the hate of Shylock, which the humanity of Shakespeare has all but excused, and has made pathetic in its frustration at the close. Thus the antitype of Marlowe's 'Barrabas' assumes a shape which has all the possibilities of tragic drama, awakening at once horror and pity.

Just when Shakespeare's own worldly success
was becoming assured, and when he had lately
produced in 'Twelfth Night' his lightest and most
graceful piece of fanciful mirth and gaiety, the clouds
began to gather round the crown and kingdom; 'the
mortal moon's eclipse' was imminent, and the poet's
friends were involved in the threatening gloom.   The
position could not be better described than by J. R.
Green in his 'Short History':—'The outer world
suddenly darkened round him.   The brilliant circle
of young nobles whose friendship he had shared was
broken up by the political storm which burst in a
mad struggle of the Earl of Essex for power.   Essex
himself fell on the scaffold; his friend and Shakespeare's idol, Southampton, passed a prisoner into the
Tower; Herbert, Lord Pembroke, a younger patron
of the poet, was banished from the court.   While
friends were thus falling and hopes fading without,
Shakespeare's own mind seems to have been going
through a period of bitter suffering and unrest.' . . .
'The joyousness which breathes through his early
work disappears in "Troilus" and "Measure for
Measure," failure seems everywhere.' . . . 'But the
very struggle and self-introspection that these
dramas display were to give a depth and grandeur
to Shakespeare's work such as it had never known
before.   The age was one in which man's temper
and power took a new range and energy.   The daring
of the adventurer, the philosophy of the scholar, the

passion of the lover, the fanaticism of the saint, towered into almost superhuman grandeur. Man became conscious of the immense resources that lay within him, conscious of boundless powers that seemed to mock the narrow world in which they moved. It is this grandeur of humanity that spreads before us as the poet pictures the wider speculation of Hamlet, the awful convulsion of a great nature in Othello, the terrible storm in the soul of Lear which blends with the very storm of the heavens themselves, the fearful ambition that nerved a woman's hand to dabble itself with the blood of a murdered King, the reckless lust that "flung away a world for love." ' . . . ' Amid the terror and awe of these great dramas, we learn something of the vast forces of the age from which they sprung. The passion of Mary Stuart, the ruthlessness of Alva, the daring of Drake, the range of thought and action in Raleigh or Elizabeth, come better home to us as we follow the mighty series of tragedies which began in "Hamlet" and ended in "Coriolanus." '

Professor Dowden's view of the same phase of the poet's activity should also be quoted : ' This period during which Shakespeare was engaged upon his great tragedies was not, as it has been sometimes represented, a period of depression and of gloom in Shakespeare's spiritual progress. True, he was now sounding the depths of evil as he had never sounded them before. But his faith in goodness had never

been so strong and sure.' [1]   He had now explored
the whole range of horrible imaginings, he knew all
the pity of it and the pathos attending on a piece of
ruined nature.   But the poet's heart *au fond* retained,
or, if you will, recovered, its profound serenity of
hopefulness and human sympathy, and was fully
aware that

> ' Consolation's sources deeper are
> Than sorrow's deepest.'

The transition from the lighter to the graver vein
is apparent in ' Measure for Measure ' and in ' Julius
Caesar.'   In ' Troilus ' there is a strain of bitterness
which vents itself in irony, and while the speeches
of Ulysses, who acts as Chorus to that drama, contain a fund of wisdom that might furnish forth ten
tragedies, the tragic note is hardly present there.
In ' Measure for Measure,' though in form a comedy,
there is a profound sadness, and the cry of Isabella,

> ' Man, proud man,
> Drest in a little brief authority
> Plays such fantastic tricks before high heaven
> As make the angels weep,'

seems to come direct from the poet's heart.   ' Timon,'
a play of uncertain date, reflects a kindred strain of
bitterness, as of a fruit that becomes acrid before it
ripens and mellows.

' Julius Caesar,' nearly contemporary with
' Hamlet,' comes first in the series of Roman plays,

---

[1] *Shakespeare's Mind and Art.*   Ed. 1901, p. 229.

and it may be convenient to treat them here together.
The ' ancient Roman honour ' was already an ideal
of native nobility in ' The Merchant of Venice,' and
in the translation by Roger North of Plutarch's
' Lives of the Great Greeks and Romans ' from the
French version of Amyot the poet found fresh
material in another sort of chronicle, dealing with a
time considered even more heroic and conceived in
a more imaginative vein. The imperial spirit now
awakened in England proudly saw its prototype
in Imperial Rome, so that his audience were well
prepared for the new theme. Shakespeare follows
Plutarch no less faithfully than he had followed
Holinshed, but the 'Lives ' were written with a
feeling for climax and proportion not equally present
in the English chronicler, and the poet has taken full
advantage of this opportunity. If Caesar were the
hero of the piece that bears his name, the unity of
action could scarcely be regarded as complete, notwithstanding the appearance of his ghost to Brutus,
and the line ' O Julius Caesar, thou art mighty
yet.' But Brutus is in reality the tragic hero ; and
the action culminates quite regularly at the end of
the third act with his flight and that of the other
conspirators after the assassination. And although
at this critical point, as before observed, Brutus is
eclipsed by Antony, the grandeur of Shakespeare's
conception of him is essentially tragic. Its truth to
Nature is convincingly brought home to any one who

contemplates the bronze bust of Junius Brutus in
the Museo delle Termine at Rome. That dark
countenance expresses the inmost spirit of the words
' It must be by his death.'   The inspiration of ancient
Rome, thus indirectly received through Plutarch,
revives, in a new manner, the rhetorical element
which was so prominent in the early historical plays;
but the rhetoric is now more consciously elaborated
and with a variety of style adapted to the several
characters. Cassius in persuading Brutus, Brutus in
his vain attempt to convince the citizens, and Antony
in the supreme effort through which he sways their
minds, have each a different style of eloquence, in
which their mental characteristics are most strongly
marked.

In ' Coriolanus ' and ' Antony and Cleopatra '
even more closely than in ' Julius Caesar,' Shakespeare treads in the footsteps of the ancient
chronicler, whom he follows incident for incident,
and often line for line. The appeal of Volumnia
and the description of Cleopatra's barge are copied
almost verbatim from Roger North.[1]   Yet the
whole is transfused with supreme imagination, and
with a spirit of the profoundest tragedy. Coriolanus is *par excellence* a tragic hero and Volumnia
a tragic heroine, although the person of Menenius
belongs to comedy and the tribunes are satirically
rendered, while the mob of citizens are once more

[1] The latter description is not in Amyot.

an unflattering mirror of the common people—the
mutable many, as imagined by the Tudor mind.
From the nature of the subject, there is an absence
of the complexity which belongs to other dramas
of the period. The person of Coriolanus has all the
' solidity of the antique.'

In 'Antony and Cleopatra,' the poet approaches
more nearly to his tragic ideal. Enobarbus, who at
the opening acts the part of a Satyric Chorus, on his
reappearance in Act IV. utters a truly tragic note,
and emphasises where it most needs to be recognised
the nobler side of Antony.   In the earlier portion of
the play in which the person of Cleopatra is so
wonderfully characterised, there is a rich vein of
high comedy, without which the drama, as a whole,
would lose much of its magnificent power.   The
same is true of the scene (with a dark background)
in which the Triumvirs are feasted upon Pompey's
barge.   The countryman who brings the asp to
Cleopatra, bears those traces of rusticity of which
Shakespeare's audience were so fond, yet the tragic
burden of his basket of figs may well check the
rising merriment that would else have marred the
pathos of the close.   A great actress must overpower
any sense of the ludicrous with the words, 'How
poor an instrument may do a noble deed,' and
but for this half page, the drama from Act III.
sc. ix. to the end has a purely tragic effect that is
unequalled except in Shakespeare.   No play of his

mature period is more characteristic of his individual genius. To call it a tragi-comedy would be to degrade it by placing it on a level with other Jacobean works that bear that name. It is a Shakespearian historical drama of the first order, developing as it proceeds into the deepest tragedy.

It would be unfair to Shakespeare's high conception of the passion of love to dwell upon the contrast between his treatment of it here and in 'Romeo and Juliet.' It may well have been that at this stage in his career he could not have recaptured the lyric intensity and perfect charm of that earlier effort. But if in the later play there is a loss of simplicity and directness and a deep sense of disillusion, there is a more comprehensive insight into the complexity of human nature. Cleopatra is not altogether kindly treated by the poet. In Plutarch she has more of queenliness and native dignity, but she does not, as in Shakespeare's play, exhibit the 'infinite variety,' the fascination and the wilfulness of a splendid and capricious woman. In the fifth act the poet, with surpassing skill, succeeds in reconciling us to a nature whose extravagances have been the cause of immense disaster. From the Roman whom she had loved deeply as well as passionately, she has at last imbibed some portion of the Roman nobleness of spirit. Octavius pays a parting tribute to 'her strong toil of grace.' Thus a sufficient cause is rendered for the ruin of a great warrior and statesman who, while contending for the empire of the world, was drawn aside by a devouring passion to defeat, dishonour, and death. The conflict of contending emotions has never been more powerfully rendered than in the fourth act of this great drama. And, as is usual with him in portraying disaster, the tragic poet reminds us of what might have been—in other words, of that ideal of life which is set off in greater brilliance by the shadow of the catastrophe.

Notwithstanding the number and variety of the scenes, the drama has a steady onward movement reaching to the height at Actium, where Cleopatra's flight makes the turning-point, and there is a subordinate crisis, a sort of ' lightening before death ' in the fight before Alexandria. The jealous passages which come between and mark the transition, of which the scene is laid, not at Alexandria (as editors have wrongly supposed), but, in accordance with Plutarch's narrative, on the coast of Peloponnesus, have a poignancy in them, and a reach of psychological insight which Shakespeare himself has hardly surpassed.

I may add a few brief notes on some minute points in the plays which have been considered in this chapter.

'The Merchant of Venice,' Act IV. scene i. line 324 :

> ' Be it but so much
> As makes it light or heavy in the substance
> Or the division of the twentieth part
> Of one poor scruple.'

It is strange that Theobald's conjecture ' on the division' has not been generally adopted. It had occurred to me independently before I knew of the suggestion, and appears no less certain than Johnson's emendation of 'Antony and Cleopatra,' Act IV. sc. xiii. line 73, ' No more, but e'en a woman' for ' No more but in a woman' of the folios.

' Antony and Cleopatra,' Act III. sc. ix. line 4:

> ' Made his will, and read it
> To public ear.'

How could Caesar's making his own will be construed as an offence to Antony? In Plutarch, Octavius takes the testament of Antonius from the custody of the Vestal Virgins and publishes it. I would propose ' Ta'en my will' and account for the corruption by the similarity of sound.

Act III. sc. xi., xii., xiii.: the headings are an invention of the editors, and are clearly wrong.

In sc. x. line 31, Canidius says:

> ' Toward Peloponnesus are they fled,'

and in sc. xiii. line 168, Antony says:

> ' Caesar sits down in Alexandria, where
> I will oppose his fate.'

That is still in the future. In Plutarch, Antony and Cleopatra, after the defeat at Actium, take refuge for a while on the coast of Peloponnesus.

The headings of Act III. sc. xi. and xiii. ought to be ' A deserted seaport in Peloponnesus,' and for sc. xii. ' Caesar's Camp,' omitting ' Egypt.'   The precarious situation adds greatly to the pathos of these scenes.   The fugitives are hanging on to safety, as it were, by the eyelids.

Act V. sc. i. line 15 : ' The round world.' To heal the metre and improve the sense, read ' The ruinated world.'   The word ' ruinate ' is not infrequent in Elizabethan English, and occurs in ' Lucrece,' 944 : ' To ruinate proud buildings with thy hours.'

CHAPTER XII

'HAMLET'

Remarks of Coleridge and Goethe criticised—The Hamlet legend and
the old play—The person of Hamlet—The ideal prince of Shakespeare in the court of Denmark—Glimpses of his earlier days—
An impossible position—'Lapsed in time and passion'—Pretended
madness—The age of Hamlet—Horatio—Laertes—Ophelia—
Claudius—Gertrude—Rosencrantz and Guildenstern—Polonius—
Fortinbras—Osric—Bernardo and Marcellus—Notes.

SHAKESPEARIAN tragedy in its highest development,
as we have seen, represents the disastrous effect of
untoward circumstances working on a great but
passionate nature endowed with high possibilities
of good, but liable to injury. In Hamlet the nature
is of the greatest, the passion of the noblest, the
possibilities of good are boundless, the circumstances
overwhelming, and the defect of quality most venial.

No student of this drama can afford to neglect
the critical observations of Coleridge and of Goethe.
Coleridge says: 'One of Shakespeare's modes of
creating character is, to conceive any one intellectual
or moral faculty in morbid excess, and then to place
himself, Shakespeare, thus mutilated or diseased,
under given circumstances. In Hamlet he seems

to have wished to exemplify the moral necessity of a due balance between our attention to the objects of our senses, and our meditation on the workings of our minds—an *equilibrium* between the real and the imaginary worlds. In Hamlet this balance is disturbed . . . Hence we see a great, and almost enormous, intellectual activity, and a proportionate aversion to real action, consequent upon it, with all its symptoms and accompanying qualities. This character Shakespeare places in circumstances, under which it is obliged to act on the spur of the moment : Hamlet is brave and careless of death ; but he vacillates from sensibility and procrastinates from thought, and loses the power of action in the energy of resolve . . . He mistakes his seeing his chains for the breaking them, delays action till action is of no use, and dies the victim of mere circumstance and accident.' Goethe's view is not dissimilar. ' Shakespeare intended to depict a great deed laid upon a soul unequal to the performance of it—as it were an oak planted in a china vase.' There is truth in both these judgments ; but there is also an element of subjectivity : they leave something out of account both as to the personality and the situation. If Hamlet had been like Coleridge, an intellectual dreamer, his failure to act would have less moved our pity ; if, as Goethe imagined, his nature had been too delicate for great achievements, he would not have inspired us as he does with admiration.   I hope to make my meaning clear by considering, first, the fable, and secondly, Shakespeare's treatment of it.

I. The Hamlet myth or legend existed before Shakespeare's time in at least three shapes: in the chronicle of Saxo Grammaticus, the historian of Juteland, written in thirteenth-century Latin; in the French tale of Belleforest, founded on the Italian of Bandello, and afterwards translated into English; and in an English drama, perhaps by Kyd, the popular author of 'Jeronimo' and the 'Spanish Tragedy.' The earlier play had been acted repeatedly during the ten years before Shakespeare's 'Hamlet' appeared, and its popularity is shown by the frequent quotation of the phrase 'Hamlet, revenge!' which seems to have been spoken by the Ghost. It appears therefore that the earlier playwright, in dramatising the tale of Belleforest, borrowed from Seneca, as other dramatists had done, this piece of celestial machinery.

There has also lately been discovered an Icelandic *saga* with a peculiar version of the same fable, but this was of course unknown to the Elizabethans, and only shows the widespread interest excited by this tale of horror.

Shakespeare probably drew his materials from the earlier play,[1] though he may have glanced also

---

[1] That traces of the old play remain in the Quarto of 1603 may be inferred from some passages which do not appear to be corrupted and yet are not in Shakespeare's manner. For example, the speech

at Belleforest, but as the old play is lost we must go
back to Saxo and Belleforest for the data which are
presupposed.

Hamlet's father had conquered Norway and
England, and had married Geruth, a distant kins-
woman. The King's brother, envious of his triumph,
had murdered him, and married his queen. Young
Hamlet was determined on revenge, and to cover
his design, like Brutus under the Tarquin, or David
at Gath, he pretended to be insane. But the King

of Ophelia in relating to her father the manner of Hamlet's farewell
begins as follows :

> ' Oh young Prince Hamlet, the only flower of Denmark,
> He is bereft of all the wealth he had,
> The jewel that adorned his feature most,
> Is filched and stolen away, his wit's bereft him,'

and more on the same level until the touch of Shakespeare
comes in :

> ' He seemed to find his way without his eyes ;
> For out of doors he went without their help,
> And so did leave me.'

Still more convincing is the Queen's speech in Act III. sc. iv.
line 136, where the following lines occur, of which Mr. Grant White
says, ' I do not believe that they were written by Shakespeare ' :

> ' Alas it is the weakness of thy braine,
> Which makes thy tongue to blazon the heart's griefe ;
> But as I have a soule, I sweare by Heaven,
> I never knew of this most horrid murder :
> But, Hamlet, this is onely fantasie,
> And for my love forget these idle fits ! '

This is not like the garbling of a pirate, and certainly it is not
Shakespeare's.

suspected him, and sought to entrap him in three ways :

1. By contriving a private interview between him and his mother, whilst a subservient courtier was hidden behind the tapestry or under the straw. Hamlet perceived the trick, slew the courtier, and reproached his mother.

2. His enemies set as a decoy a young maid who loved him, but he held to his purpose, so that this too was in vain.

3. He was sent on a mission to England, then tributary to Denmark, with companions who bore secret orders for his death. He discovered the plot on shipboard, and substituted an order for his companions' death, sealing it with a duplicate of the royal signet. After adventures in England which do not concern us, he returns to Denmark, and with deep cunning overpowers the courtiers, whom he has made drunken at a festival, after which he beheads the King. Then he harangues his countrymen, and ascends the throne.

There is a sequel to the story which again concerns us not.

II. The fatal catastrophe, the Ghost, the play within the play, and the premature return from England, which is necessary to the plot, were in all probability anticipated in the earlier drama. What then, it may be asked, remained for Shakespeare to invent? The answer may be given in the blunt

language of the late Professor Freeman, ' only everything.' If the old play had survived we should have
felt in comparing it with our ' Hamlet' as we do in
examining the drama of ' King Leir and his Three
Daughters,' which preceded Shakespeare's ' Lear,'
that the genius of Shakespeare shone forth more
brilliantly and appeared more marvellous than ever.
How this has been effected is Shakespeare's secret,
but the heart of the mystery is obviously to be sought
in his conception of the personality of Hamlet.
He has transmuted the cunning plotter of Saxo and
Belleforest into a prince after his own heart, endowed with genius, accomplished in all the culture of
the Renaissance, not professing philosophy, yet comprehending more of the wisdom of life than many
philosophers, and ready to acknowledge that ' there
are more things in Heaven and earth than are
dreamt of in your philosophy.' He is a youth whose
powers of action when called forth by clear occasion
are far in advance of his years, but at the same time
a youth of genius, who is ever reaching towards the
ideal, and gifted with an impassioned nature, which
under happy auspices might have reformed the world,
but when foiled and turned aside takes refuge in
irony and outward cynicism.

The person so conceived is placed in the rude
environment which is presented in the old legend,
' benetted round with villanies,' defrauded of his
proper right and of the scope belonging to it, and

having his best feelings outraged by the conduct of
those who should have been his nearest and dearest
friends. The Hamlet of Shakespeare's predilection,
planted in the Denmark of the story—therein lies
the gist of the drama. Were we to invert Goethe's
image and say that Hamlet is the oak sapling set in
a coarse and narrow vessel of cast iron, we should
come nearer to the truth. For Hamlet is no weak-
ling. The pathos lies in the contrast between what
he might have become, and the ruin caused by
circumstances and the wickedness of others, working
on his own powerful and refined but passionate
nature. If we turn again to Coleridge's notion—
apart from the fallacy of supposing Shakespeare to
start from an ethical preconception—it is true that
Hamlet's mind is thrown back upon itself, and that
his utterances are tinged 'with the pale cast of
thought'; but the preponderance of speculation over
action is the result not of Hamlet's nature only, but
of his environment reacting on his nature. One of
the greatest charms of the drama is supplied by
those passages in which we are allowed to perceive
something of what Hamlet was before the blight of
circumstance had fallen upon him. We see this in
his manner to Horatio, his companion at Wittenberg, and to the players, whose performances he had
enjoyed in happier days; and also in his remembrance
of Yorick, recalling the brilliance of the elder Hamlet's court. What underlies all else in the person of

Hamlet is natural affection combined with a keen
and lofty sense of honour. It is the outrage done
upon these qualities ' in the morn and liquid dew of
youth ' that makes the pathos of the situation. That
one of such a princely nature, of a heart so golden,
of such deep tenderness, so accomplished in all that
might have adorned a throne, should find himself
in such a world, his father murdered, his mother
corrupted, his hopes for life destroyed, his love
embittered, and nothing left to live for except the
doubtful and desperate purpose of a questionable
revenge, to be followed inevitably by his own destruction—that is the tragedy. The circumstances
are such as to render effective action impossible,
and therefore to preclude all action on the part
of one who ' looks before and after ' as Hamlet does.
Considerations infinite prevent him from forming
a distinct and well-prepared plan. For, first of all,
however deep the impression made on him by the
apparition, he is a child of the Renaissance, and
his conception of the supernatural is tinged with
scepticism. Before staining his conscience with
blood-guiltiness, he must have grounds more relative
than this. And if he is to act securely, with whom
should he conspire? With Horatio? That would
be the ruin of his best and only friend :—with
Laertes? His own act has rendered that impossible :—with Rosencrantz or Guildenstern? The
very suggestion is ridiculous; he knows them too

well. To act alone, as he clearly sees, is to seal
his own doom. Yet, being now convinced of his
uncle's guilt, and rightly suspecting that he has
overheard the colloquy with his mother, he thinks
to stab him in presence of the queen, and by mis-
adventure kills Polonius instead. That hastens his
exile and precipitates the plot against his life in
which his two friends are the accomplices. On
discovering this he acts with promptitude and un-
hesitating resolution. The engineer is hoisted with
his own petard, and when, favoured by circumstances,
the Prince returns to Denmark, he would have
watched his opportunity, but his purpose is again
frustrated through the blood-feud with Laertes.
His heart will not suffer him to take the King at
his prayers, but his final resolution has been made ;
and when the plot against him has at last succeeded
and he is wounded mortally, he resolutely stabs the
usurper, and forces on him the poisoned bowl. This
he does not merely in self-requital but in the determined execution of a long-meditated resolve. The
act so long contemplated is now trebly justified, and
motives which have impelled him towards it, but
were hitherto foiled by external obstacles and mental
scruples, have now accumulated into a compelling
cause which is fully approved by reason. Even at
that crowning moment—and this reveals at once the
depth and the practical wisdom of his unique personality—he shrinks from the misconstruction which

must inevitably follow his most rightful deed, unless his one friend survives him, to report his cause aright to Denmark and to the world.

> 'O God! Horatio, what a wounded name,
> Things standing thus unknown, shall live behind me!
> If thou didst ever hold me in thy heart,
> Absent thee from felicity a while,
> And in this harsh world draw thy breath in pain
> To tell my story.'

The loving reverence for his father's memory is continually apparent. It breaks forth even through the cynical irony of his conversation with Rosencrantz and Guildenstern, and his cruel banter of Ophelia in the play scene. It is the one thing that holds him true to his ideal. His faith in womanhood is doubly shattered, his love is ruined, although deep within him it still smoulders, ready when challenged to burst into flame. His friendships all but one have proved hollow and treacherous. That he should retain his belief in the 'divinity that shapes our ends,' in the 'special Providence about the falling of a sparrow,' attests not only the depth of his nature, but the strength of that main motive that is so rich within his soul. The places where this motive of filial duty comes out most vividly are the scene at court (Act I. sc. ii.), the colloquy after the departure of the Ghost, and his apostrophe to his father's apparition in the closet scene.

That in Hamlet the native hue of resolution suffers from the 'pale cast of thought,' that when

he acts he does so on the impulse of the moment
and not out of any settled plan, is undeniable. But
the ' vicious mole of nature in him ' is not merely
the excess of intellectual activity ; the contemplative
mind is steeped in passionate emotion. That quality,
which is inseparable from every tragic personality,
contains the germ of great failure as well as of great
success :

> '. . . The dram of base
> Doth all the noble substance oft subdue
> To his own scandal.'

It is because, had fortune favoured him, he would
have lived to achieve nobly, and to act beneficently,
because the splendid powers of action which he
shows occasionally would have grown to some
magnificent result, that our compassion for him
equals our admiration. Such is the verdict of Fortinbras : ' For he was likely, had he been put on, to
have proved most royally.'

But he was ' lapsed in time and *passion*.' The
circumstances which most effectually foil his purpose
—the death of Polonius, hastening the voyage to
England, the death of Ophelia, the quarrel with
Laertes—all rise out of the passionateness of his
nature, which has been rendered more impetuous
through being suppressed.

There is no use in watering down the part of
Hamlet. His open contempt for Polonius, even
when dead by his hand, the fitfulness of his succes-

sive moods in the graveyard, the lightness with which
he regards the fate of Rosencrantz and Guildenstern,
his old companions whom he has sent to their
deaths : all this, if it needs excuse, may be excused,
but should not be dissembled. Repressed emotion
in the recoil may commit ravages, without the
shadow of remorse. Hamlet is no mystic, no senti-
mentalist, but a tragic personality. In other words,
he is at once passionate and noble.

His madness is, of course, pretended, as in the
old story ; but, first, he is a consummate actor, and
his pretence of madness is therefore extremely like
reality ; secondly, it is a convenient screen for his
ironical humour ; and thirdly, although he is throughout profoundly rational, yet his whole nature has
been overstrained and wrenched, and the consequence,
in an organism so emotional and so delicately hung,
is a condition of unstable equilibrium. This accounts
for the few critical moments when he loses self-
control to the ruin of his purpose, and for his harsh
behaviour and even brutality, especially towards
Ophelia. Those who think this strange know little
of the effect of outraged affection in an agonising
crisis upon a young and ardent soul.

There is another point which in this connection is worth considering. The play of 'Hamlet,'
although the most perennially interesting, is not
the most mature of Shakespeare's works ; and it
is not unreasonable to suppose that in moulding

it he may have left some part of the old material imperfectly assimilated. The assumed madness which belonged to the tradition had been crudely treated in earlier versions of the story, so as to be hardly distinguishable from real madness. And our poet, in representing the simulated insanity which is alone consistent with his creation, may have now and then allowed the simulation to verge too closely on reality. At the same time, that such a mind as Hamlet's could be temporarily unhinged by the onslaught of the terrible disasters which agonised him, is undoubtedly part of Shakespeare's view. An ironical bitterness would then be the only mode in which one so tried could be relieved of the perilous stuff that weighed upon the heart. Coleridge perceived this when he said : 'Hamlet's madness is made to consist in the free utterance of all the thoughts that had passed through his mind before— in fact, in telling home-truths.'

The interview with Ophelia was forced upon him, after he had bidden her a last farewell. He suspects the motive of it, and his feeling turns to a strange blending of honey and gall. But his yearning tenderness for her who is now placed beyond the reach of his protection betrays itself even amidst the outward harshness.

A trivial question has been raised about the age of Hamlet. Yorick's skull has been in the ground 'Three and twenty year.' Hamlet had ridden on

his back, say, as a boy of seven; that would make
him thirty in the graveyard scene. The First Quarto
says 'twelve years,' taking off eleven, and making
Hamlet's age nineteen. Was this alteration made
by Shakespeare? To my mind both this and the
other question about the time occupied by the action
are rather futile. They occur to readers of the
play, but not to the audience. And it was of the
auditor, or spectator, that the poet thought. A
great tragic action has little to do with precise de-
terminations of time. Hamlet, when the play begins,
is in his first youth, just returned from the Univer-
sity; in the fifth act he is no longer so young. This
is as it should be. The pathos of the earlier scenes
turned largely on the youth of one upon whom such
overwhelming responsibility had fallen; but it is
otherwise with the catastrophe. After all that has
passed, within him and without, he is no longer
'in the morn and early dew of youth.' There is a
similar alteration in Macbeth. When he first comes
on we see him in the pride of manhood, 'Bellona's
bridegroom lapp'd in proof.' But at Dunsinane his
'way has fallen into the sear, the yellow leaf,' and he
feels himself on the threshold of old age. It matters
not that the plot only gives room for months not
years; it is enough that much has happened outwardly and still more within the spiritual sphere.
The spectator has not time to reckon days and
weeks as he is carried along from scene to scene.

Another trifling question has been excitedly
discussed. What does Gertrude mean in the last act
by saying that her son ' is fat and scant of breath ' ?
Some say that Burbage, who first acted the part,
was fat and pursy. I believe it simply means that
the Prince was out of training, having ' forgone all
custom of exercises,' as he told Guildenstern ; and I
am glad to find myself confirmed in this opinion by
Mr. Craig, the Oxford editor, as quoted in Dowden's
edition of ' Hamlet,' p. 237. ' Mr. Craig understands
fat to mean not reduced to athletic condition by a
fencer's training.'

I have elsewhere spoken of the value for the
tragic dramatist of the contrast between the passionate hero and some strong but unimpassioned personality who plays a secondary part, like Ulysses
in the ' Ajax ' or Theseus in the ' Oedipus Coloneus.'
For Hamlet, amidst all the agitation, suspense, and
disillusionment surrounding him, there is one point
of repose and strength in the friendship of Horatio,
' the man that is not passion's slave.' This is
probably one of the few elements of the plot that are
of Shakespeare's own invention. To accentuate the
fact that Hamlet is a son of the Renaissance, he is
sent to school at Wittenberg, and one of his fellow
collegians comes to visit him at Elsinore. The
difference between them is well marked at the opening of the platform scene. The Prince, unaccustomed

to exposure, and shuddering inwardly with spiritual anxiety and awe, is chilled by the night wind and says with a shiver, 'The air bites shrewdly, it is very cold'; to which Horatio calmly and almost cheerily replies, 'It *is* a nipping and an eager air.' He has no superstitious fears; and though on the actual appearance of the ghost he trembles and looks pale, yet he immediately recovers his self-possession, and confronts the apparition as Banquo the weird sisters. The poet has been at great pains to indicate the cool moderation of Horatio's mind :— 'A piece of him'—'has this thing appeared again to-night?'

'A mote it is to trouble the mind's eye '——
'So have I heard and do *in part* believe it.'

'While one with moderate haste might tell a hundred.'
('Longer, longer!') 'Not when I saw it.'

And when Hamlet after his exultant outburst on making the great discovery says : 'Would not this—get me a fellowship in a cry of players, sir?' his friend answers quietly 'Half a share.'

This toning down of thought—this habit of understatement, throws into relief the excitement of the protagonist. And although on the platform Hamlet cannot confide the secret to his best friend, yet in the sequel it is evident that he has unbosomed himself completely: 'You do remember all the circumstance?' 'Remember it, my lord?'

Laertes is another person probably invented by

Shakespeare and in another way contrasted with the hero, while, unlike Horatio, he contributes something to the *dénouement*. Although short of princely, he is a gentleman as the times go—not a scholar or a student, but outwardly accomplished; what Matthew Arnold called *l'homme moyen sensuel*. Unintentionally, though by his own act, Hamlet becomes the object of Laertes' revenge. And Laertes is worked upon by the King to take a mean advantage against the slayer of his father. His cause is like Hamlet's, as the Prince acknowledges, but his manner in prosecuting it is different. He has the same fiery indignation in a lower form, but not the large discourse to apprehend the consequences of immediate action, or the sensitive conscience that asks for adequate evidence of guilt, before execution; nor yet the scrupulous virtue that shrinks from violence where not clearly justified. Laertes is the foil to Hamlet, setting in a vivid light his soul of honour, his far-reaching thoughtfulness, his tenderness, his sublime spirit of equity. Hamlet is complex but noble, Laertes is simple but not free from baseness.

Of poor Ophelia there is little to say. Although her fate might have filled up an ordinary tragedy, it is rather her want of character than any positive characteristic that gives her significance in the drama. Yet Hazlitt was right in saying: 'Oh, rose of May! Oh, flower too soon faded! Her love, her madness, her death, are described with the truest touches of tenderness and pathos. It is a character which nobody but Shakespeare could have drawn, and to the conception of which there is not the smallest approach, except in some of the old romantic ballads.'—Hamlet's love for her is well accounted for by Dr. Hudson : ' Ophelia is the only pure, sweet, honourable form of humanity about the court; and Hamlet naturally craves communion with her as a relief from the oppressive, sickening foulness of the place. She is the one sole beam of light and joy in his social whereabouts, and his clear, earnest eyes cannot forgo the solace of that.' Simplicity has an irresistible charm for a soul that is wearied with complexity. Ophelia is the most passive amongst Shakespeare's women ; and what renders her mad scenes so pathetic is their utter unconsciousness. The blood-curdling screams which we have sometimes heard from her on the stage are not only unpleasing, but most untrue. ' Her death was doubtful,' says the priest; but the Queen's narrative shows it to have been accidental.

And Gertrude—she has all a woman's frailty, but she has not lost all her womanliness, and she is still a mother. In the First Quarto, as probably in the old play, she promises to be her son's accomplice in contriving the death of her second husband. This was a false note; it was corrected in the Quarto of 1604. The poet spares her in this ; and she is too weak to be entrusted with such a design, although

Hamlet's secret is safe enough with her for very shame. Even the usurping King, in spite of his ingrained villiany, has touches of the double nature which makes the pathos of 'Macbeth'; compare for example—

> 'There is no shuffling, there the action lies
> In his true nature, and we ourselves compelled
> Even to the teeth and forehead of our faults
> To give in evidence—'

with

> 'this even-handed justice
> Commends the ingredients of our poisoned chalice
> To our own lips.'

Rosencrantz and Guildenstern, the hollow friends, are slightly sketched. They are unpitied in their deaths, and Hamlet's callousness on the subject is intelligible. A passionate mind under the pressure of one great grief is coldly indifferent to much that would otherwise affect it.

Polonius is a trimmer and a time-server, but not so contemptible as he is sometimes represented. He is what the vicissitudes of the Danish court have made him. In better times under the former King, his policy, though shallow enough, may have been useful to the State. As Coleridge puts it, he 'is throughout the skeleton of his own former skill and statecraft.' And though he is now body and soul subservient to the crown, he seems once to have had a shrewd outlook upon life, and even to have formed for himself a code of prudential morality which he bequeaths to his son. 'To thine own self be true,

&c., is the highest note, which father and son both
fail to realise in practice.

There are other figures which stand in the background and serve to link the action to the world at
large—the Ambassadors, the Norwegian captain, and
Fortinbras, who again makes an effective contrast to
Hamlet, not in character but in position. He is free
from the entanglements which have ruined Hamlet's
career. His final entrance rounds off the play, as is
done in Shakespeare's other tragedies, when the
passions of the scene are exhausted, and we are
brought back into the light of common day.

Osric, the vain courtier, serves to sustain Hamlet's
ironical attitude towards those without, in contrast to
the solemnity of his intimate converse with Horatio.
Elsewhere, in ' Romeo and Juliet,' ' Othello,' ' Macbeth,' and ' Lear,' the comic persons are removed as
the tragic interest deepens towards the close.

Even Bernardo and Marcellus, who treat Hamlet
as a prince, while he insists on treating them as
friends, and Francesco the honest soldier, have each
a distinct individuality and contribute to the totality
of the effect. The remarks of Coleridge on the
opening scene are worth remembering. ' It has
been with all of them as with Francesco on his
guard alone in the depth and silence of the night :
" 'Twas bitter cold and they were sick at heart, and
not a mouse stirring." The attention to minute
sounds—naturally associated with the recollection

of minute objects and the more familiar and trifling
the more impressive from the unusualness of their
producing any impression at all—gives a philosophic
pertinency to this last image; but it has likewise its
dramatic use and purpose. . . . That Shakespeare
meant to put an effect in the actor's power in the
very first words, " Who's there ? " is evident from the
impatience expressed by the startled Francesco in
the words that follow, " Nay, answer me, stand and
unfold yourself." A brave man is never so peremp-
tory as when he fears he is afraid. Observe the
gradual transition from the silence and the still
recent habit of listening in Francesco's " I think
I hear them " to the more cheerful call out which a
good actor would observe in the " Stand ho ! who is
there ? "

'Bernardo's inquiry after Horatio, and the repetition of his name in his own presence, indicate a
respect or an eagerness that implies him as one of
the persons who are in the foreground, and the
scepticism attributed to him :

> " Horatio says, 'tis but our fantasy;
> And will not let belief take hold of him "

prepares us for Hamlet's after eulogy of him as one
whose blood and judgment were happily commingled.
The actor should also be careful to distinguish the
expectation and gladness of Bernardo's " Welcome,
Horatio!" from the mere courtesy of his " Welcome,
good Marcellus ! " '

The tragedy of 'Hamlet' recalls the words of Brutus in 'Julius Caesar,' which were written about the same time :

> 'Between the acting of a dreadful thing
> And the first motion, all the interim is
> Like a phantasma, or a hideous dream.
> The genius and the mortal instruments
> Are then in council, and the state of man,
> Like to a little kingdom, suffers then
> The nature of an insurrection.'

I add a few notes on minute points.

Act I. sc. iv. line 37 :

> 'Doth all the noble substance of a doubt
> To his own scandal.'

The passage is absent from the First Quarto, and from the Folios, so that the text depends wholly on the authority of the Quarto of 1604. The point to be observed is that 'To his own scandal' is not added in further explanation, but is in construction after some verb which lurks under the corruption. I have long since suggested 'oft subdue,' comparing the language of Sonnet cxi. lines 6 and 7 :

> 'And almost thence my nature is subdued
> To what it works in, like the dyer's hand.'

'The dram of base' (the most probable emendation) 'brings all the noble substance under the influence of its own ill-repute: the true metal is tainted in estimation through the admixture of a

little alloy.'   Supposing the types to have been
shaken and the ' s ' to have dropped out, the letters
o, f, d, e, u, b, t, might suggest to an ingenious com-
positor the reading ' of a doubt.'

Act II. sc. i. line 115, ' Cast beyond ourselves.'
Is not this a metaphor from a questing hound over-
running the scent ?

Act III. sc. i. line 67, ' Mortal coil ' is of course
rightly explained as ' trouble or turmoil of mortal
life.'   A strong emphasis should be laid on ' mortal '
in opposition to an *immortal peace.*

Lines 89 to 92.   As the scene is commonly acted
the change in Hamlet's manner is unaccountable.
The actor addresses Ophelia in a tone of gallantry
either serious or ironical, which in neither case har-
monises tolerably with what precedes and follows.
I understand the passage thus :

Line 89.   Hamlet, who had imagined himself
alone, now catches sight of Ophelia, who with her
prayer-book is at the back of the stage.   His old
passion for the moment revives, and he apostrophises
her in these words, which are spoken aside.   She is
unaware of this.

Line 90.   To his astonishment after what has
passed (Act II. sc. i. 77 to 100), she, in obedience to
her father, comes forward and accosts him.

Line 92.   He is revolted, and his suspicions are
aroused.   He replies as if he were a stranger and a
madman.

Line 133. His suspicion has worked itself into clearness, and he puts this home question. Ophelia's manner of answering is conclusive : his rejoinder is more embittered, and he speaks louder, that eaves-droppers may overhear. (See above, p. 121.)

Act V. sc. i. line 119. ' A pair of indentures ' : is there not a double meaning here, viz. ' dints with a spade ' ?

Sc. ii. line 129. 'You will do it, sir, really.' Horatio compliments Hamlet on his proficiency in the fashionable jargon.

CHAPTER XIII

' MACBETH '

Not a villain in grain—The double nature—Dramatic foreshortening—Development of personality—Sources of the fable—The
witches—Lady Macbeth and Banquo—The third murderer—
Apparition of Banquo the main crisis—Macduff the avenger—
World-weariness—The porter—The sergeant.

In the three great tragic masterpieces which remain
to be considered there is a distinct advance, not
indeed in the conception of human character, but in
artistic creation, in concentration of interest, and
steady climax. In the poignancy and depth of
sympathetic emotion no dramas produced before or
since have been equal to them. Shakespearian
tragedy now assumes its final shape.

Just as Hamlet has been imagined to be a mere
dreamer, so Macbeth has been represented as from
the first radically and irredeemably bad. That is to
degrade the rôle of Shakespeare's protagonist into a
mere character part, which when prolonged through
five acts becomes intolerably monotonous; like an
air with variations played upon a single string.
The psychological development, the interaction of
personalities upon one another, the inward conflict

and dis-harmony attendant on a double nature, the
fatal consequences of a first step in crime, are all
ignored.

Let unity of character by all means be maintained.
But when the character is a rich and complex one,
the interest consists in observing the effect of
circumstances in bringing out this or that element
into full realisation. What we care to watch and
sympathise with is not a dead uniformity but a living
growth. Hazlitt remarked on the extraordinary
versatility of a genius which could create two such
different types of ambition as Richard III. and
Macbeth ; but the difference lies not only in the
types themselves but in the change that a dozen
years had made in Shakespeare's mind and art.

Here we encounter a preliminary objection. It
is said that Macbeth had clearly planned the murder
before the beginning of the play, else how could
Lady Macbeth reproach him with having broken the
enterprise to her ? This happens on the evening of
the day when she has received his letter announcing
his meeting with the witches. A literal interpreter
is puzzled to find time for the interview so alluded
to. He may be equally puzzled, supposing Macbeth
to have previously made the suggestion to his wife,
to account for his soliloquy when the witches
vanish :

> ' This supernatural soliciting
> Cannot be good, cannot be ill,' &c.

Such an interpreter has failed to realise what is meant by dramatic foreshortening. The poet had to present a complex action which must have occupied years and make it the two hours' business of his stage. And he has presented it in all its aspects continuously and as a whole. Fortunately for the illusion which it is his business to produce, his audience, in receiving a rapid series of impressions, have not time to ask themselves 'but how can such a thing have happened between this and that?' And yet it must be supposed to have happened if the plot is to be complete.

Some breaks and pauses on the other hand which contribute to the main effect are too often neglected. Between Duncan's arrival and Macbeth's first soliloquy there is sometimes no change of scene. Yet the King arrives on the calm evening of a long summer day, when the castle, silhouetted against the twilight sky, shows the martins flitting round their nests in the turrets and gables; whereas the following scene opens at the commencement of the fatal night, while Duncan is at supper and sewers are carrying dishes across the stage. It is then, by the glimmering torchlight, that Macbeth comes forth and soliloquises :

' If it were done,' &c.

The words of Stendhal not inaptly describe the chief person : ' Macbeth, a man of honour in the first act, led astray by his wife, murders his benefactor

and his king, and becomes a monster of wickedness.'
Such an account is inadequate, but it at least
acknowledges the truth that there is a vast difference
between the warrior as we see him at the opening
and the tyrant at the close of the play.   At his first
entrance he is a brave and gallant chieftain, who has
nobly served his king and country and receives the
meed of honour which is his due. He is keenly
alive to the ' golden opinions ' which are showered
upon him from all kinds of people ; he appreciates
the graciousness of Duncan, the meekness with which
he has borne his great faculties ; and he has himself
a comprehensive vision of human good and ill.
Partly to engage our sympathies, with which no
tragic hero can dispense, and partly that by the
lurid light of his guilty consciousness we may see
the action in its true nature, the poet has gifted
Macbeth with a portion of his own power of
imagination.

Like all who are thus gifted, he is sensitive to
every breath of praise or blame, and to all outward
influences, including the sway of intimate affection.
Nor, when roused to action, is he without firmness
and persistence of resolve.   In a less turbulent age,
in a constitutional State, where the crown was not
synonymous with absolute power—if otherwise
mated, or if removed by birth from all expectation of
the throne, such a nature might have passed through
life, if not as a model of exalted virtue, yet with

well-deserved distinction and untarnished name. But there is in him, unknown hitherto even to himself, a lurking demon of ambition, which, once awakened, all the better counsels of his higher nature, all his knowledge of the world, his love of approbation, his milk of human kindness, his imaginative visions of the better life, are powerless to control or to repress. In this he differs from Banquo, who is exposed to similar temptations but is almost unaffected by them. The will of Macbeth is swept along on that fierce current, and it must be owned that he struggles but feebly against it. Yet it is the presence in him of this double nature that sustains our interest. Like Marlowe's Dr. Faustus, he scarcely ever loses consciousness of the hell within him, and with that consciousness we sympathise. We are reminded of Horace's confession ' I see and approve the right : I follow the wrong,' and still more of the Medea of Euripides :

> ' I know how evil are my deeds to be ;
> But passion rules all else within my breast,
> Passion, the cause of mightiest ills to men.'

Shakespeare is well aware that ' No man all at once becomes most base '; and he has shown the horror with which Macbeth contemplates the first suggestion of crime ; how, after entertaining it, he shrinks back again and would leave all to chance ; and then once more takes refuge in fatalism—'Che sarà sarà';

> ' Come what come may,
> Time and the hour runs through the roughest day.'

We are left in doubt whether the murder would have been consummated but for the counsel and assistance of Lady Macbeth, and for the opportunity of Duncan's visit, which for the moment only renews Macbeth's hesitation. But in the meantime his ' flighty purpose ' has been precipitated by the designation of Malcolm as prince of Cumberland, which marks out Duncan's eldest son as the immediate heir. This, which forms part of the original legend, makes it necessary for Macbeth, if he would gain the crown, ' to take the nearest way.'

Shakespeare still derives his fable from Holinshed, but treats it with far greater freedom than he had used in the history plays. In the murder scenes he has woven together the assassination of Duncan at Inverness with that of King Duff by Donwald and his wife in their castle at Forres. It is from this that all relating to the two chamberlains is taken. From a single phrase of the chronicler's he has created the part of Lady Macbeth. He has cleared Banquo of all complicity in the crime, not only, as Brandes thinks, because he was the ' father of our kings to be,' but with a view to dramatic contrast. He has omitted the ten years of good government attributed to Macbeth. And of ' the women in strange attire, supposed to be the weird sisters,' he has made—what we all know.

'They are wholly different from any representation

of witches in the contemporary writers, and yet
presented a sufficient external resemblance to the
creatures of vulgar prejudice to act immediately
on the audience' (Coleridge). 'He took enough of
current and traditionary matter to enlist old credulity
in behalf of agents suited to his peculiar purpose,
representing to the age its own thoughts, and at the
same time informing that representation with a
moral significance suited to all ages alike' (Hudson).
Compare the treatment of the Erinyes by Aeschylus.
However they may have appeared to Shakespeare's
contemporaries, for us, and in reality for the poet
himself, the witches are but the embodiment of the
temptation. Shakespeare had attained to an unrivalled contemplation of the workings of the human
spirit, and he had also gained the most complete
mastery of the method of his art. In his interpretation of the legend, making use of the prevalent
belief in the supernatural, he was enabled not only
to invest the action with an atmosphere of horror
and a mysterious feeling of sublimity, but to visualise
spiritual conceptions, so as to bring them home
directly to the apprehensions of an audience whose
minds were comparatively rude. Psychological facts
are thus embodied in a concrete form. The 'air-
drawn dagger' which Macbeth sees in vision is an
expedient of a cognate kind : such in a still higher
degree is the apparition of Banquo.

Lady Macbeth's influence is of a different order.

Her narrow and concentrated volition, roused into
intense activity by her affection, conspires with the
dark impulse which has already gained the ascendency in her husband's thoughts. Devoted to his
interests as she conceives them, and sympathetically
fired with the ambition of sharing with him the
splendour of a crown, she is reckless of all else for
the time. Unlike her husband, she is wanting in
imagination ; or rather her imagination, vivid as it
is, is wholly occupied with the direct means towards
a definite end. In pursuing this she is able to sup-
press all ulterior considerations, all ' compunctious
visitings ' of her woman's nature, overborne as these
are by the determination to screw her husband's
courage to the sticking place. Once, indeed, the
sight of Duncan as he lies asleep reminds her
of her father. That human touch is worthy of
Shakespeare. But it is important to observe that
at the moment when she owns to this she is alone.
It is only during the brief interval of Macbeth's
absence that she betrays any signs of perturbation.
When he is present, her self-possession is complete,
and is contrasted throughout with the ever-recurring
flurry into which he is cast by the reaction of his
better nature. Some have actually taken those
thrilling words ' Macbeth doth murder sleep '—' but
wherefore could I not pronounce Amen ? '—for
mere hypocritical maundering. That is to ruin
the part of Macbeth as surely as Lady Macbeth's

part is ruined if she is permitted, except for the brief space above indicated, to waver in her self-control.

Another contrast of prime importance is that between Macbeth and Banquo. In Banquo there is seen the princely heart of innocence, the spirit of unattainted loyalty, the religious mind that abhors even the thought of evil. He cannot avoid indeed having a well-founded suspicion of Macbeth, who sounds him, but finds him incorruptible:

> ' It shall make honour for you.'—' So I lose none
> In seeking to augment it, but still keep
> My bosom franchised and allegiance clear,
> I shall be counselled.'

But he shakes off this and other gloomy impressions, until the death of Duncan leaves no reasonable doubt. Then he recalls the promise of the weird sisters to him, and wonders if it might not set him up in hope. That is the only hint the poet gives from Banquo's side, of the situation which makes it impossible that he should live. And it is a touch of nature, showing that even Banquo's virtue is not superhuman.

Lady Macbeth's criminality is exhausted in the one great act, in which she had laboured to promote what she believed to be her husband's good and his deep though half-expressed desire. She is not directly an accomplice in the death of Banquo. The idea of it has floated before her mind, and to comfort her husband she remarks of Banquo and Fleance that 'In them Nature's copy is not eterne.' But beyond this she is not the co-agent with Macbeth in anything that follows.

Shakespeare's fine tact is shown in this as in his treatment of the Queen in 'Hamlet,' and there is another reason which will be stated presently.

It has been doubted whether in the scene after the murder Lady Macbeth really faints, or only seems to faint. May not both be in a manner true? The swoon is well timed to distract attention, but being aware of this, she may have allowed herself to go, and the last straw that overpowers her is Macbeth's avowal that he had killed the grooms. She had fully reckoned on Duncan's murder, but had not bargained for more blood, and the killing of the grooms (an incident in the original story) was not a crime merely but a blunder. From a dramatic point of view her fainting is a preparation for the sequel, revealing the woman's nature which had been suppressed in her but not extinguished. In the third act she has recovered her composure, and with presence of mind, rendered more absolute by her prosaic temper, she does her best to obviate the dangerous consequences of her husband's distraction. But he no longer communicates his inmost thoughts to 'his dearest partner of greatness.' The golden round when once attained brings only 'curses not loud but deep' in which she must partake with him.

She feels the consequences of his guilt, but has no
longer any share in his designs. She is more and
more alone; the feminine temperament, which she
had violently held down in the supreme hour of her
ambition, now asserts itself independently of the
will; and when sleep has put her off her guard, her
thoughts involuntarily return to the hour of her
most intense volition; impressions of pity, fear, and
horror, which she then made nothing of, react on
the enfeebled brain. The sleepwalking scene is the
result. At last, just when the toils are closing round
Macbeth, she utterly despairs, and 'By self and
violent hands' takes off her life. We pity her the
more because the world at large regards her as 'his
fiendish queen.'

Meanwhile Macbeth has been supping full with
horrors. An English theologian has observed that
'by a single act of crime an inroad is made into the
whole moral constitution which is not proportionably
increased by its repetition.'[1] But, though not proportionably increased, it is increased notwithstanding; and the stages are well marked in the tragedy
of 'Macbeth.' To the usurper's motto—'Things bad
begun make strong themselves by ill,' it may be
rejoined that they do so *seek* to strengthen themselves but fail inevitably. The first effect on Macbeth of the accomplished crime is to fill him with
mistrust. He confides no longer even in his queen,

---

[1] Jowett's *Essay on Conversion* in his edition of St. Paul.

whose clear, though limited, vision had aided him
so far, and might have saved him from much subsequent disaster. He does not know how far she is
willing to follow him, and he has enough of grace
still left to shrink from dragging her further into
the sea of blood. Banquo, the one witness of
his ambition, and Fleance, the hope of Banquo's
posterity, must be taken out of the way. But in
executing this design the tyrant again blunders
through suspicion. The escape of Fleance is due
to the third murderer, whom Macbeth has sent to
make assurance doubly sure. This departure from
the programme disconcerts and irritates the two first
employed :

> ' He needs not our mistrust, since he delivers
> Our offices and what we have to do
> To the direction just. . . .'

> ' Who did strike out the light ? '
> > ' Was't not the way ? ' . . .

> > ' We have lost
> Best half of our affair.'

Thus Macbeth is rendered more insecure than ever.
And the unavailing remorse for the unavailing crime,
though it has no power upon his will, yet harrows
him profoundly. This fact is brought before our
eyes in the great banquet scene, where the apparition
of Banquo, with its effect upon Macbeth, produces
an acme of horror rising far beyond that of Duncan's
murder, and forming the main crisis of the whole
action. In the sequel the fears and scruples which

shake him drive the usurper further and further into
a system of espionage and oppression :

> 'There's not a one of them but in his house
> I keep a servant fee'd.'

And the one chieftain who, remaining in Scotland,
had preserved an attitude of independent patriotism,
the Thane of Fife, who had avoided the coronation
and refused the banquet, flies to England to join
with Malcolm in petitioning the English King
(Edward the Confessor) to send a force with them
from the north of England to oppose the tyrant.
Others in Scotland who know of this are cherishing
a secret hope

> ' That by the help of these—with Him above
> To ratify the work—we may again
> Give to our tables meat, sleep to our nights ;
> Free from our feasts and banquets bloody knives,
> Do faithful homage and receive free honours:
> All which we pine for now.'

Thus all is ready for the *dénouement*. The avenger
is already arming, and only one thing is yet wanting
to sharpen his sword. Macbeth's better genius has
finally forsaken him : he has no more regrets for the
past, no yearning for lost innocence—only a gloomy
but resolute outlook on the future. At the opening
of the fourth act we see him as his crimes have
made him—a denaturalised monster, living only for
evil, and blinded to all good.

> ' The magnet of his course is gone and only points in vain
> The shore to which his shivered sail shall never stretch again.'

For the milk of human kindness there is fierce and undiscriminating hatred, for such tender imaginings as ' Pity like a new-born babe,' a mind that revels in images of cruel horror :—

> ' Though nature's germens tumble all together
> Even till destruction sicken ' :—

for the clear vision of the consequences of his deeds, an ear that ties itself to the equivocation of the fiend, and such blind fury of purposeless cruelty as shall arm the avenger with tenfold malice. The suggestions of the tempter no longer ' make his seated heart knock at his ribs.' Instead of that he is on the most familiar terms with those powers of evil whom he thinks to command when he is really their slave. He hates them—for hatred is now his second nature—but he conspires with them, for he is resolved to know by the worst means the worst. What a revelation of a ruined and darkened soul appears in his opening words to the weird sisters in their cave—

> ' How now, you secret, black and midnight hags,
> What is't you do ? '

That disclosure, more than any glamour of witch-craft, is the motive of the cauldron scene; and at the end of it, on hearing that Macduff, whose murder he had last been meditating, is fled to England, he determines on that hideous butchery which seals his own final doom, while for the

audience it infuses a strain of pity into the tragic
horror.

There is a yet further change. The tyrant's
reign is becoming unendurable. All hearts are
alienated. The speech of Ross (who at first had
followed Macbeth), in breaking the dreadful news to
Macduff, discovers a condition of the commonweal
which cannot last. But the state of Macbeth's own
mind is still more ruinous. He has become callous
to all feeling except a dull recurring sense of things
irrevocably lost—'As honour, love, obedience, troops
of friends.' That is the form in which some echo of
his better mind comes back to him. For he is more
and more isolated. The wife, who at the first onset
had faced the music more firmly than himself, has
broken down under the accumulated guilt, and his
chief anxiety about her is the fear that she may
reveal too much :—'Cure her of that!' The only
being with whom he has any human relation is the
physician—who has been drawn to Dunsinane by
the hope of profit and is longing to get away. It is
now that Macbeth gives utterance to those expressions of world-weariness, the finest in any language,
and of the longing for oblivion, which have sometimes earned for Shakespeare the false accusation of
pessimism. The dreariest of all these utterances is
drawn from him by the death of the Queen. The
only emotion which the sudden news awakes in him
is one of impatience that it should have happened

now, when he has so much to strive against, and not afterwards when he might have leisure to endure the loss, and it might even have been in some ways a relief. Then, commenting on his own indifference, he meditates on the nothingness of life :

> ' She should have died hereafter . . .
> To-morrow and to-morrow and to-morrow.' . . .

But the instinct of the tried warrior is once more roused in him when 'Birnam wood is come to Dunsinane,' and with the fitful courage of despair, instead of remaining on the defensive, he goes forth into the field to fight against overpowering numbers. Many lives are sacrificed to his savage valour—the brave young Siward's amongst the rest. With one man only he does not choose to fight. The blood of Macduff's wife and children sits heavy on his soul, and he avoids him. But the Avenger finds him out, explodes the confidence of the tyrant in the magic charm; and, when threatened with exposure as a public show, the shielded warrior 'tries the last' and like some hunted animal dies game.

Whether anything of ' gag ' has been added to the Porter's speech to please the 'groundlings' has been a question in dispute since raised by Coleridge; but the part of the Porter is invaluable. He lets in for a moment some common daylight upon the dreadful night, and interposes an indispensable break between the horror with which the knocking is heard within and the cheerful unconsciousness of those without, including the destined Avenger.

The part of the Sergeant has also been questioned, but is it not necessary to the exposition, corresponding to Othello's speech to the Venetian senate?

For hints of the 'double nature'—too often slurred over by the actor of Macbeth—see especially II. ii. 75; III. ii. 22–35; and for premonitions of the sleep-walking scene, II. ii. 35, 36; III. ii. 6, 7.

CHAPTER XIV

' OTHELLO '

Construction of ' Othello '—Increased concentration—Coleridge on the catastrophe—Iago's soliloquies—Comparison with Cinthio's ' Moor of Venice '—The handkerchief—The recall of Othello—The fourth act—Appendix to Chapter XIV.—Note.

IN the three great masterpieces of his maturity, Shakespeare touches a supreme height at once of psychological insight and of dramatic art. These dramas are replete with the wisdom of life, with knowledge of mankind, and far-reaching apprehension of the possibilities of good and evil, while the presentation alike of character and situation is extremely concentrated, and is so ordered as to give the uttermost effect to the main action. There is no florid rhetoric, as in the historical plays; no exuberance of description or narrative but what is profoundly calculated to drive the impression home. And this increasing condensation, which gives greater firmness and continuity to the dramatic structure, is not due in any way to a rule imposed from without, like that which clipped the wings of

Corneille's natural freedom and impoverished, while
it polished, the productions of French tragic drama.
It arose entirely from the uncompromising seriousness with which the poet now confronted his mighty
task, and the inward intensity and energy of his
earnest thought, 'too full for sound and foam.'   The
poetic style undergoes a corresponding change.
Without dwelling on technicalities of versification,
it is enough to compare alike the joyous and the
melancholy notes of ' Romeo and Juliet' with corresponding passages of ' Macbeth' and 'Othello.'   In
these there is nothing to remind us of either lark or
nightingale ; the lyric strain has vanished and there
is little of elegiac softness ; but the poetic quality is
not less absolute.   It is only more inward and more
intense.   There is the same creative power in both,
but the creation is of a different order ; the tragic
tone now dominates all.   Ben Jonson may well
have had Shakespeare in his eye when he wrote of
his Virgilius in 'The Poetaster' :

> ' And for his poetry, 'tis so *rammed with life*
> That it shall gather strength of life with being
> And live hereafter, more admired than now.'

The plot of ' Othello' is woven with extraordinary skill.   Even the precise Dr. Johnson has
remarked that ' little or nothing is wanting to render
the " Othello " a regular tragedy.'   He suggests,
however, that the play should have opened with the
arrival of Othello in Cyprus, the previous scenes at

Venice being thrown into the form of narrative, so as to preserve the unity of place. This pedantry would have deprived us of Othello's stately vindication of himself before the Magnificoes, in which his nobleness is revealed, and of the scenes between Iago and Roderigo, ending with the soliloquies of Iago, in which he developes his infernal plan. Shakespeare's judgment in opening the play as he has done needs no further defence.

Othello is the Moor of Venice : that is given amongst the data of the fable. Shakespeare takes advantage of it to make possible what in any case might seem an improbable course of events. Othello has done great service for the State in war, but is a novice in the arts of peace. Desdemona's love for one much older than herself, of a different race, and quite absorbed in great affairs, has a touch of strangeness which helps to excite his passion for her, but also can be made a ground for doubting her constancy. The simplicity of the Moor is no match for Italian subtilty. His warm temperament, in which passions once excited have a tinge of animalism, is associated with a strain of superstition which may give to his emotions, when much roused, an exaltation equivalent to an imperative law. These elements, and others akin to them, are wrought together into a whole of which the stupendous reality is irresistible. Over against the tragic error which subdues him, is set the background of a glorious career, in which, fighting for the Christian against the Turk, he had rolled back the advancing tide of barbarism.

Coleridge has a subtle note on the catastrophe, which, however, leaves out (I venture to think) the strain of latent ferocity which is interwoven with essential nobility in the complex character of the Moor.

'Othello,' says Coleridge, 'does not kill Desdemona in jealousy, but in a conviction forced upon him by the almost superhuman art of Iago : such a conviction as any man would and must have entertained who had believed Iago's honesty as Othello did. We, the audience, know that Iago is a villain from the beginning, but in considering the essence of the Shakespearian Othello we must perseveringly place ourselves in his situation, and under his circumstances. Othello has no life but in Desdemona, and the belief that she, his angel, had fallen from the Heaven of her native innocence, wrought a civil war in his heart. . . . As the curtain drops, which do we pity the most?'

The truth perhaps lies somewhere between the thought expressed in this fine passage, and another which recognises the twofold personality of the Moor; between the panther-like strides of Salvini and the attitude of proud severity assumed by Tamagno, the great singer, in the last act of Verdi's opera : Justice with her sword.

In order to account for the otherwise incredible

perversion of Othello, the character of Iago, the cunning, malignant, low-minded Italian, is wrought out with marvellous power. In order to impress this upon the audience, Shakespeare has recourse to those soliloquies in which the villain comments on his own malignity in a manner which reminds us of Gloster's description of himself in the opening of ' Richard III.' In making Iago characterise his reasons as ' divinity of hell,' perhaps the poet oversteps the limit of psychological truth, for the Italian has no double nature such as we find in Macbeth ; he is unrepentant throughout, more irredeemable even than Edmund in ' Lear.' That Iago ' has a grain of conscience ' is the one amongst Lord Tennyson's criticisms to which I am inclined to demur. His utter blackness sets off the splendour of his victims. But the conventional expedient, as it is not this time used in dealing with a tragic hero, but only with a secondary person, may be defended on the ground of necessity. It is not quite true, however, that Iago's villainy is altogether motiveless. His confession to Roderigo, although it is made with a purpose, is not therefore to be imagined as groundless, and the reasons which he adduces may not be thought inadequate for a coarse and unscrupulous, but strong-willed and subtle-minded Italian as conceived by an English dramatist about the year A.D. 1610. Iago has no hankering after better things like Macbeth. He is utterly reprobate.

His knowledge of the world does indeed include the knowledge of good, but the good has no attraction for him, his knowledge of it only makes him a more accomplished hypocrite ; and the poet has availed himself of this, so as to accentuate the misery of Othello, in language to which Shakespeare has not scrupled to add touches of poetic beauty.

The comparison of the drama with the original fable is peculiarly instructive in the case of ' Othello.' Almost all the incidents which occur in Cinthio's narrative have afforded hints which may be recognised in the play ; but they are developed, altered, transposed, transfigured, with the most absolute mastery. The persons of ' Disdemona ' (the ill-starred), the Moor, the Ensign or ancient (*alfiero*), the Lieutenant (*capo di squadra*), the Ensign's wife, the courtezan, all come into the story, but excepting Disdemona they are nameless. The person of Roderigo is developed from that of the soldier for striking whom the Lieutenant is cashiered. In an appendix to this chapter the chief parallels, which prove the poet's intimate acquaintance with the novel, are collected in one view. Two points call for special notice here : (1) the use made of the stolen handkerchief, and (2) the recall of Othello.

(1) The handkerchief, in the story as in the play, is the Moor's bridal gift. It is embroidered with the finest Moresco work (*lavorato alla Moresca sotti-lissimamente*) : this Shakespeare developes into the

magic mysteries of Act III. sc. iv. lines 56-76.
The Ensign steals it from Disdemona's girdle while
she is playing with his child—Iago is not imagined
as having children, that would spoil the part—he
places it in the Lieutenant's bedroom, without his
knowledge, and tells the Moor that Disdemona had
given it to the Lieutenant. The Moor questions
Disdemona and from her blushes infers the worst.
She talks to the Ensign's wife about it, who warns
her to avoid suspicion. The Lieutenant gives it to
a woman skilled in embroidery to be copied, and the
Moor sees it in her hand. This woman Shakespeare
has identified with the courtezan who is mentioned
afterwards in the story in connection with another
incident. It is needless to point out the extraordinary subtilty and power of judgment with which
the poet has woven these crude suggestions into the
most critical moment of his plot.

(2) In the Italian tale Othello is recalled in consequence of the murder of Disdemona, of which he
is accused by the Lieutenant on false information
from the Ensign. Shakespeare does not account for
the recall. The audience are left to imagine some
intrigue of the Magnificoes, perhaps of Desdemona's
kinsmen ; he turns it into the occasion of Othello's
final outburst in Act IV.

The whole of this fourth act is a triumph of
dramatic construction. In no other tragedy has the
sequel of the main crisis been presented with such

telling force.   The interest is not only deepened but sustained at the height.

Othello's passion has been wrought to fever point and the catastrophe is certain.

> ' Like to the Pontick sea,
> Whose icy current and compulsive course
> Ne'er feels retiring ebb,'

his bloody thoughts will ne'er look back, till that a capable and wide revenge swallow them up.   At the opening of Act IV. we see how the man is altered and denaturalised, like Macbeth in the cave scene, and he is maddened by witnessing Cassio's laughter and seeing the handkerchief in Bianca's hand.   But that is not all.   The commissioners unexpectedly arrive from Venice with the mandate for Othello's recall, and the appointment of Cassio in his room.   Desdemona, still at cross purposes, is glad of it.   She knows that the war is over, and is longing to return to Venice, where she imagines her father to be still alive.   She rejoices too, quite innocently, on Cassio's account, and is relieved to think that her importunity is no longer required.   If it is strange that she should not realise the wound to Othello's honour, the audience have been prepared for this obtuseness in an earlier scene—Act III. sc. iii. line 84, when Othello says :

> ' I will deny thee nothing :
> Whereon, I do beseech thee, grant me this,
> To leave me but a little to myself.'

This fresh turn of affairs, directly clinching the catastrophe, may be compared with the murder of Macduff's wife and children in 'Macbeth.' But the action here proceeds more straightforwardly, and no one can find the fourth act of 'Othello' tedious, as Dr. Ward confesses to have found the fourth act of 'Macbeth.'

APPENDIX TO CHAPTER XIV

Shakespeare's *Othello*.	Cinthio's *Moor of Venice*.
	(In Hazlitt's Shakespeare's Library Ed. 1875. Part I. Vol. II. pp. 285–308.)
Act I. sc. i. line 69. 'Incense her kinsmen.'	P. 308. Finalmente fu da' parenti della donna, come egli meritava, ucciso.
Act I. sc. ii. line 5. 'I had thought to have yerk'd him here under the ribs.'	P. 294. Se io non avessi temuta l' ira vostra, gli avrei dato, quando cio mi disse, quella mercede, coll' ucciderlo, della quale egli era degno.
Act I. sc. iii. lines 250 ff. 'That I did love the Moor to live with him . . . Let me go with him.'	P. 285. Tratta non da appetito donnesco, ma dalla virtù del Moro, s' innamorò di lui. . . . P. 287. Vogli' io venire con voi, ovunque andrete.
Act II. sc. i. lines 68–73. 'Tempests themselves . . . do omit Their mortal natures, letting go safely by The divine Desdemona.'	P. 288. Con somma tranquillità del mare, sen' andò in Cipri.

Act II. sc. i. lines 196–202.
'The heavens forbid
But that our loves and comforts should increase
Even as our days do grow . . .'

P. 288. Con un affettuoso bacio le disse :—Iddio ci conservi lungamente in questo amorevolezza, moglie mia cara.

Act II. sc. iii. line 154.
'Striking Roderigo.'
Ibid. line 251.
'Cassio, I love thee,
But never more be officer of mine.'

P. 290. Il Moro, per aver messo mano alla spada il capo di squadra, nella guardia, contra un soldato, e dategli delle ferite, lo privò del grado.

Act III. sc. iii. line 39.
'I cannot think it
That he would steal away so guilty-like.'

P. 297. Il capo di squadra, udita la voce del Moro, temendo ch' egli non scendesse a danno suo, senza rispondere parola si diede a fuggire.

Act III. sc. iii. line 45.
'If I have any grace or power to move you,
His present reconciliation take.'

P. 291. Molte volte aveva tentato di rappacificare il marito con lui.

Act III. sc. iii. line 197.
'Look to your wife, observe her well with Cassio.'

P. 291. Se terrete aperti gli occhi, voi stesso lo vi vedrete.

Act III. sc. iii. line 229.
'Not to affect many proposed matches
Of her own clime, complexion, and degree.'

P. 293. Come colei, a cui già è venuta anoia quella vostra nerezza.

Act III. sc. iii. line 263.
'Haply for I am black.'

Act III. sc. iii. line 291.
'This was her first remembrance from the Moor.'

P. 298. Gli ha ella donato quel pannicello da naso, che voi, quando la sposaste, le deste in dono.

Act III. sc. iii. line 361.
' Give me the ocular proof.'

Pp. 294–5. Se non mi fai, disse, vedere cogl' occhi quello, che detto mi hai . . . meglio per te sarebbe, che tu fossi nato mutolo.

Act III. sc. iii. line 376.
' O wretched fool !
That livest to make thine honesty a vice.'

P. 294. Poi che tanto oltre mi ha portato il debito mio, ed il desiderio dell'onor vostro . . .

Act III. sc. iii. line 398.
' It were a tedious difficulty.'

P. 295. Non mi potrà essere se non malagevole.

Act III. sc. iv. line 31.
' I think the sun where he was born
Drew all such humours from him.'

P. 292. Voi Mori siete di natura tanto caldi (association *per contra*).

Act III. sc. iv. lines 56 ff.
' That handkerchief
Did an Egyptian to my mother give.' . . .

P. 296. Il qual pannicello era lavorato alla moresca sottilissimamente.

Act III. sc. iv. line 179.
' Take me this work out.'

P. 301 (una donna in casa) . . . Prima ch'ella l' avesse, si mise a farne un simile.

Act IV. sc. i. line 28.
' Cannot choose
But they must blab.'

P. 294. L' ha detto a me, come quegli, cui non pareva la sua felicità compiuta, se non ne faceva alcuno altro consapevole.

Act IV. sc. i. line 142.
Ha ! ha ! ha ! '

P. 298. Parlandogli di ogni altra cosa, che della donna, faceva le maggiori risa del mondo.

Act IV. sc. i. line 215.
' Get me some poison.'

P. 303. Discorrendo l' uno con l' altro se di veleno, o di coltello si devea far morir la donna.

Act IV. sc. i. line 229.
Enter Lodovico.

P. 308.   I Signori Vene-
ziani . . . fecero dar delle mani
addosso al Moro in Cipri, e
condurlo a Venezia.

Act V. sc. i. line 25.
(Iago from behind wounds
Cassio in the leg and exit.)

P. 302.   Gli dirizzò un
colpo alle gambe, per farlo
cadere, ed avenne, ch' egli
tagliò la destra coscia a
traverso.

Act V. sc. i. line 73.
Bianca.

Ibid. Uscendo . . . di casa
di una meretrice, colla quale
egli si sollazzava.

Act V. sc. ii. line 304.
' Torments will ope your lips.'
   Ibid. line 368.
' The time, the place, the
   torture : Oh, enforce it.'

P. 308.   Fu messo al
martorio anco l' alfiero per
paragone.

Note on I. i. 21. ' A fellow almost damned in a fair wife.'
I propose to read ' in a fair outside.' Cassio is ' framed to make
women false.' Compare Ford's *Broken Heart*, II. i. :

' Why, to be fair,
Should yield presumption of a faulty soul.'

CHAPTER XV

'KING LEAR'

THE late Mr. Mark Pattison once said, 'The more I read the ancient classics, the more impossible I find it to be to write about them.' A similar feeling may well oppress the mind in endeavouring to write or speak about our own greatest classic. Despair of saying anything to the purpose is aggravated by the quantity of what is daily said. It is not now as in the time of Johnson or even of Coleridge. The charm of the subject is inexhaustible, but the temptation to enjoy in silence is very strong.

> 'Not that the summer is less pleasant now . . .
> But that *wild* music burthens every bough,
> And sweets grown common lose their dear delight.'

The Shakespearian student who feels that he has something to say is further embarrassed with a sense of the comparative deadness and futility of all

written comment.   If Plato, in his prime, experienced
this with regard to the expression of philosophical
ideas, how much more must the same reflection
hinder the attempt to analyse these living forms of
supremely creative imagination !   Life itself is hardly
more complex, yet there is here an added element of
concentrated artistic unity.   Sympathetic readers
may enter into the poet's meaning, great actors may
in part interpret him ; but the would-be interpreter
who sits down, pen in hand, how should he not
swerve from direct and simple intuition ?   How not
mar his own impressions in striving to communicate
them ?

If Shakespeare's judgment in his maturest work
is to be anywhere questioned, it is in the management
of the rise and fall.   It may be alleged, perhaps,
that the climax is sometimes too rapid, and that,
before the turning-point arrives, the action has
mounted to an elevation from which descent is
perilous.   Shakespeare certainly lays a heavy task
on his protagonists, and the burden of it is felt most
severely in the fourth act.   But before admitting the
full force of such an objection one should have seen
each play complete upon the stage, which is hardly
possible.

In ' Lear,' which Charles Lamb thought unact-
able, the difficulty is enhanced by the condition of the
modern spectator, on whom the wonderful display of
full-blown madness in Act IV. can hardly produce its

just effect after the exhaustion of his sympathies by the heartrending scenes in the castle of Gloucester, and upon the heath.   Nor, on the other hand, does the subject of 'Lear' afford the opportunities which are so splendidly used in 'Antony and Cleopatra' and 'Macbeth,' for sustaining the intensity of dramatic action to the end.   Lear's deeds are, as he himself implies, more in suffering than in act, and pathos is the chief note throughout.   As to the interweaving of comedy with tragedy, that crux of the Elizabethan stage, the Fool's part (some bits of manifest 'gag' being discounted) is confessedly a triumph of skill ; but the Fool, like Ismene in the 'Antigone' of Sophocles, disappears when the play has culminated, so that the chief actor has not to contend in the later scenes, as the actor of Hamlet has, with such interlocutors as the first Gravedigger and Osric. The gradation of feeling is no less masterly than the portrayal of character.

It may be confidently maintained that, in his maturity at least, Shakespeare absolutely preserves what may be called emotional consistency.   Any want of keeping in the inward movement, from scene to scene, such as is sometimes apparent on the stage, may safely be referred to the actors, and not to him.   But there is another kind of unity or consistency of which he has been less careful.   He knows that the attention of the audience at any given time will be engrossed by the action immediately

before them : and he has sometimes, with apparent
wilfulness, enhanced the effectiveness of a particular
moment, by neglecting minute data that are given
or implied elsewhere. An obvious instance occurs
in ' The Merchant of Venice ' (I. ii. 135) where, after
six suitors have been described as on the eve of
departure, the servant announces that ' the four
strangers' are seeking Portia, ' to take their leave.'
And in the first scene of the same play (I. i. 70) it is
assumed that Lorenzo, Bassanio, and Antonio are
to dine together—clearly *not* at Bassanio's, as the
reminder comes from Lorenzo. Yet afterwards (II.
ii. 180), when the loan has been effected, Bassanio
figures as the host. These discrepancies are evident
to those who read and re-read the printed page.
But the audience do not pause to count upon their
fingers, nor do they ask for explanation of an
arrangement which the change of circumstances
renders manifestly natural. Before censuring such
inaccuracies or repining over them, it is necessary to
take into account the conditions of performance—
particularly on the Elizabethan stage.

The extreme care which Shakespeare evidently
spent on the composition of ' King Lear ' has not
prevented some apparent flaws of this kind, which
interpreters have, as usual, attempted to gloss over.
When Regan, after her husband Cornwall's death,
has vainly tried to intercept her sister's letter to
Edmund, she is goaded into defiance, and says to

Oswald, whom she finds thus 'duteous to the vices of his mistress' (IV. v. 23) :

> 'I know your lady does not love her husband;
> I'm sure of that; and at her late being here
> She gave strange oeillades and most speaking looks
> To noble Edmund.   I know you are of her bosom.'
>
> Oswald.   'I, madam!'
> Regan.   'I speak in understanding; you are, I know it,
> Therefore I do advise you, take this note;
> My lord is dead; Edmund and I have talked:
> And more convenient is he for my hand
> Than for your lady's: You may gather more.
> If you do find him, pray you, give him this,
> And when your mistress hears thus much from you,
> I pray, desire her call her wisdom to her.'

With desperate policy, she takes the serviceable villain into her confidence, and urges him, in Goneril's interest, to save his mistress from her own infatuation by secretly favouring Regan's comparatively lawful and 'convenient' suit. According to the obvious meaning of the words, when taken with their context, she puts into his hand some written communication, which, on the grounds stated, she first advises him and then entreats him to deliver. But when Oswald is slain, only Goneril's 'letters' are found upon him: therefore Johnson and others would have us believe that 'take this note' here means 'take note of what I am going to say,' and that 'this,' four lines lower down, is some unrecognisable token. But the fact is that Shakespeare, while choosing this way of revealing Regan's passion, has not, therefore, chosen to load unnecessarily (and so to weaken) the incidental scene where Edgar, in defence of Gloucester, fells the rascal steward with his club.

This example may help to illustrate the truth that, in Shakespearian interpretation, the immediate context is more important than what is more remote. The solution of a difficulty should generally be worked out within the limits of the individual scene. Yet, though so near at hand, the clue is not always easily found. One cause of such perplexity lies in the neglected fact that the words are, after all, only one part of the affair, lying flat upon the page, until vitalised and substantiated by action. And the trouble has sometimes been aggravated rather than cured by stage traditions, in which ease of rendering will sometimes supplant effectiveness. Other causes of obscurity and error, such as obsoleteness of words and idioms, contemporary allusions, ignorance of the materials on which the poet worked, may be to a great extent removed by antiquarian and philological learning, and by a careful study of the sources of the plot. But, after all, the question will return : 'What was the poet's dramatic intention here and here?' And the answer may often turn, not on any point of laboured investigation, but on the reference of words of which the meaning is absolutely simple : 'How do you?' 'So.' 'See, see.' 'No life!'

Some analysis, in the light of these remarks, of

the action of 'King Lear,' III. ii., iv., vi. may not be unacceptable.

III. ii. 69 : 'Where is this straw, my fellow?'

Lear thus addresses Kent—supposed to be his servant Caius—who had not spoken of 'straw' in mentioning the hovel. The words of Cordelia should be compared (IV. vii. 38) :

> 'And wast thou fain, poor father,
> To hovel thee with swine, and rogues forlorn,
> In short and musty straw?'

The poet does not subject the aged King to this degradation. When they come to the hovel, Lear manifests a strong disinclination to enter it ; for which he accounts by the fine thought—

> 'This tempest will not give me leave to ponder
> On things would hurt me more.'—(III. iv. 24.)

The Fool, whom he persuades to enter first, comes forth again in crazy terror at seeing the disguised Edgar, whom Kent then summons forth, while he calms the Fool's excitement by taking his hand. This further delays the action until the approach of Gloucester with news of more suitable shelter at the farmhouse. Lear, in his fascination for Edgar, is still on the point of following him into the hovel, when Kent's advice that the King should be allowed to 'take the fellow' with him to the farm brings to an end the episode of the heath.

Thus, while Lear remains throughout upon the stage as the central figure, the outward pivot of the

action is afforded by the hovel. That revolting
refuge is the goal both of rest and of humiliation,
which, throughout these scenes, is continually
approached, but never reached. The natural repugnance of the King's mind to such vile shelter, the
fierce determination to accept the situation imposed
on him by filial ingratitude, and the effort to bring
thought in aid of resignation are all expressed in the
few words :

> ' Where is this straw, my fellow ?
> The art of our necessities is strange
> That can make vile things precious.   Come, your hovel ! '

The fourth scene may now be considered more
in detail. III. iv. 4 :

> ' Wilt break my heart ? '

The sight of the hovel chafes Lear's ' impatience ' to
the utmost. That straw is the visible symbol of
ingratitude, and sets the outraged father's heart on
fire. Under such dominance of feeling that would
be alone with itself, any practical urgency becomes
intolerable. The lightest touch from without,
especially the touch of kindness, presses with an
effect of agony. Words are not then measured by
the occasion. It may be, too, that the affectionate
insistence of his lately hired servant enhances by
contrast the cruelty of his own flesh and blood,
and thus seems to aggravate the burden that is
threatening to ' break his heart.'

During the outburst which follows, Kent stands
by and patiently awaits the subsidence of passion.
Under this steadying influence, Lear is somewhat
tranquillised, and when again addressed with the
same words, replies considerately and meekly. No
longer wholly self-absorbed, he recovers his kingly
courtesy, and says to Kent (his servant), III. iv. 23 :

> ' Prithee, go in thyself, seek thine own ease,'

adding the reflection

> ' This tempest will not give me leave to ponder
> On things would hurt me more,'

which shows that the stress of feeling is for the time
relaxed.   Then (as Kent with perfect tact remains
still and silent), overcoming at last the physical
repugnance which has mingled with all the precedent
emotion, Lear turns to enter that low door. But
no, not yet ! The Fool must have shelter first, and
he himself may remain a little longer alone with the
' contentious storm.' The current of his thoughts
is changed, however ; a rush of gentler feelings comes
over him ; he thinks with pity of the poor (III. iv.
27, ' You houseless poverty ! ').   The Fool still hesi-
tates ; but his master prevails on him with the
excuse that he wishes, as usual, to say his prayers
before going to rest.   And his ' prayer ' is the well-
known meditation on the wants of the poor—too
beautiful to garble, too familiar to be quoted in full.
It may be not superfluous, however, to observe that
the significance of the phrase ' looped and windowed

raggedness' (l. 31) is apt to be lost through the
obsoleteness of the word 'loop' as used to signify
'an opening.' The rents in the poor man's raiment
let in the weather like the slits and perforations in
an outer wall.

Edgar's voice is now heard from the hovel, and
the Fool runs out in crazy fear of him. Kent takes
the 'innocent's' hand to steady him, and bids the
supposed maniac to come forth. Edgar then enters
in his disguise. Lear is at once fascinated with this
spectacle of 'unaccommodated man.' His incipient
madness is aggravated by this new stimulus, and
the scene is thus occupied until the approach of
Gloucester—the storm continuing unabated.

Some remarks on Edgar's *rôle* may be for the
present reserved. We are still concerned with Lear.
III. iv. 130.

> *Kent.* 'How fares your Grace?'
>
> *[Enter Gloucester with a torch.*
>
> *Lear.* What's he?'

Gloucester's approach is first observed by the
Fool, who calls Lear's attention to the light, with
'Look, here comes a walking fire'; while Edgar, in
his assumed part as Tom o' Bedlam, interprets the
supposed will-o'-the-wisp to be 'the foul fiend Flib-
bertigibbet.' What ideas, meanwhile, are coursing
through the partially disordered brain of the King?
A light approaching from the castle! To face them
again, Regan, Cornwall, Goneril! Better even the

hovel, far better the storm on the open heath, than that! He becomes visibly agitated, which accounts for Kent's gentle inquiry, and, on the nearer approach of the torch-bearer, asks in the exalted tone of mental excitement, 'What's he?'

It may be observed, by the way, that in these earlier scenes the King's utterances, however wild, are always prompted by something in the immediate present. This is not equally so during the paroxysm at the farmhouse, where the maniacal impulses from within are gathering strength, and hardly at all in the fourth act, where the mental disorder has become confirmed.

III. iv. 176.

Glo. 'I do beseech your Grace——'
Lear.   'O, cry you mercy, sir!'

In the conduct of the latter part of this scene, two things are specially noticeable: the care with which Edgar is separated from his father on the stage, and Gloucester's confidential communication to the disguised Kent.

On Gloucester's entering and demanding their names (in his authority as Lord of the 'Manor), Edgar betrays his uneasiness by throwing more excitement into his 'counterfeiting,' of which he forces the pace; and, as if to keep his father at bay, ends with, 'Beware my follower. Peace, Smulkin; peace, thou fiend.' After this, he subsides almost into silence, but yields to the humour of Lear,

who draws him into imaginary conference, while
Gloucester, instead of at once importuning Lear to
go, wanders (as if insanity were catching) into a
confession of his own distraction to Kent (the supposed manservant), little knowing the innocent cause
of it (Edgar) to be so near; at the same time
hinting, what is news to the audience, that Lear's
daughters seek his death, and adding, 'Ah, that
good Kent! He said it would be thus.' After these
singular colloquies in separate groups, the renewal
of the storm recalls Gloucester's thoughts to Lear.
The King then begs pardon for his inattention, but
insists on being accompanied by Edgar, who in this
strait resorts to his single cry of 'Tom's a-cold,'
and, at Gloucester's bidding, shrinks back towards
the hovel—whither Lear (in his insane infatuation)
would have followed him, had not Gloucester been
persuaded by Kent to let Edgar come too. But
Gloucester, not relishing such company, bids Kent
(as Caius) to take the Bedlam on with him, while
he himself (thus kept apart from his son) accompanies the King.

The assumed part of Edgar, with its familiar
spirits, its snatches of folk-song, its allusion to
popular customs, is necessarily obscure; but with
the help of 'Harsnet's Declaration,' and other literature of the time, most difficulties of this kind have
been cleared away. One word of poor Mad Tom's,
however, 'Sessa,' III. iv. 103, vi. 78, remains a blank

to readers of Shakespeare as 'Selah' is to English readers of the Psalms. Without dogmatising, I should suggest that it may be a corruption of (Fr.) 'C'est ça!' and add that the exclamation of Lear in IV. vi. 207, where he runs off the stage, crying, 'Sa, sa, sa, sa,' may be an adaptation of (Fr.) Ça, ça, ça, ça![1]

'Loo, loo' (III. iv. 79) was in Shropshire forty years ago, and may be there now, and elsewhere for aught I know, the customary cry in coursing to signal to the greyhound that a hare was in view. Such customs are not of yesterday, and it may well be that the same cry is here transferred by Edgar to his imaginary chase after the fiend.

Can anything be made of his less articulate cries? 'Says Suum, mun, ha, no, nonny' (III. iv. 102) may be an attempt to express in writing, the effect of chattering teeth. 'Do de, do de' (III. iv. 59) appear to be sounds expressive at once of idiocy and cold. But such notions (or impressions) must not be urged too far.

One more suggestion may, however, be ventured. Edgar's counterfeiting (which, as has been seen above, is somewhat marred by his father's presence), although capricious, cannot be altogether lawless. One expression (iv. 57) 'to ride . . . over four-inched bridges, to course his own shadow for a traitor,' contains a pretty obvious allusion to his recent

---

[1] Compare Cyril Tourneur, *Revenger's Tragedy*, V. i.

dangers and escapes ('I heard myself proclaimed,' &c.). 'Child Rowland to the dark tower came' has a ring of genuine despair, like 'I am at the worst.' 'Thy cold bed' recalls the discomfort of the hovel. Can it be that the snatch about the Dauphin betrays a thought of Edmund, the accepted heir, and that 'let him trot by' is equivalent to a despairing 'let him have his way'? (*A propos* of the words 'I am at the worst,' it may be noted, in passing, that the phrase in IV. i. 26, 'I am worse than e'er I was,' is wrung from Edgar, not by the first sight of his father poorly led, but by the subsequent discovery that he is blind.)

In Act III. sc. vi. at the farmhouse to which Gloucester has brought the King from the heath, the first acute paroxysm of insanity breaks forth. Between the stage direction '*Exit Gloucester*' (l. 6) and the next speech of Kent, there is a piece of action occupying about two minutes, and leading up to the imaginary trial of Goneril and Regan. I know not what may be the tradition here, but it surely deserves to be noted in our books that Kent accompanies Gloucester to the outer door, and through his temporary absence the stage is left wholly to the three 'madmen' (Edgar's position rendering him helpless), so that the only controlling influence is for the time removed. To the Fool's question, suggested by the presence of Edgar, 'Whether a madman be a gentleman or a yeoman?'

Lear answers with unbridled vehemence, ' A king, a
king ! ' the piteous consciousness o his own condition
here passing off into the pride of the insane. He
takes no notice of the Fool's rejoinder, but, fired with
Edgar's demonology, conceives the design of bringing ' a thousand, with red burning spits,' to the aid
of his revenge. And having returned to the main
theme, his daughters' guilt, he resolves to bring them
up for judgment. At this point his madness is in
full career: ' nothing is ' for him ' but what is not ';
the Bedlam's blanket becomes the ermine of a judge ;
the Fool shall be his wise assessor.

The court is set; the prisoners are arraigned.
The delusion is now complete. He has them there,
and breaks forth on the accused with impotent
triumph, ' Now, you she-foxes ! ' When all this is
realised, it becomes apparent that the words of
Edgar, ' Look, how he stands and glares,' are not
addressed to an imaginary fiend in his assumed part
of poor Mad Tom, but are an *aside* of the true
Edgar expressing his astonishment and grief at the
sudden change in the appearance of the King. And
the gentle words of Kent : ' How do you, sir ? Stand
you not so amazed ! ' sufficiently indicate his surprise
and concern at the state of matters which he finds
on his return. Realising that things have passed
beyond his control, he watches patiently and
anxiously, consenting even to sit as one of that
strange ' Commission.' After the acme of Lear's

'rage,' which all but betrays Edgar into forgetting his part, Kent addresses an appeal to the King's true self (adverting to III. ii. 37, 'I will be the pattern of all patience'), but, for the time, in vain. The paroxysm spends its force. Lear falls from rage to self-commiseration, then returns to musing on the hardness of Regan's heart, and, lastly, wanders feebly back to his fancy for Edgar and his 'Persian attire.' Kent perceives the opportunity, and at last prevails on his master to lie down and rest upon the cushions. The poor King imagines himself at home and going to bed as usual (III. vi. 89).

'Make no noise, make no noise; draw the curtains: so, so, so. We'll go to supper in the morning. So, so, so.'

The words 'So, so,' in Shakespeare, Ben Jonson, &c., often accompany some *business* of a practical kind. Paulina wrapping up the child before she leaves it ('Winter's Tale,' II. iii. 130); Apemantus watching the salutations of the courtiers ('Timon,' I. i. 256); Othello 'mercifully' despatching Desdemona ('Othello,' V. ii. 89); Antony directing Cleopatra how to arrange his armour ('Antony,' IV. iv. 28); the queen in 'Cymbeline,' as her ladies finish gathering the flowers ('Cymbeline,' I. vi. 82); Prospero laying aside his magic garments, while Ariel helps to attire him in his ducal robes ('The Tempest,' V. ix. 6) are instances in point. In the present passage Kent, as Lear's body-servant, is arranging

the pillows, while his master, perhaps, hands to
him his girdle and outer garment. (Compare *infra*
IV. vi. 177, ' Pull off my boots—harder—harder
—so.') Dimly conscious of exhaustion, yet too
fatigued for appetite, Lear waives the question
of food, which just occurs to him, with the touch-
ingly incoherent words, ' We'll go to supper in the
morning.'

The profound sleep which follows offers the last
hope of restoration. But this is tragically destroyed
by the re-entrance of Gloucester with the news of
the proscription of the King. Kent takes him in his
arms, and the Fool (in his last exit) ' helps to bear
his master,' who, as Kent feels, must not be deprived
of his only remaining solace. The words of Kent
(III. vi. 105),

' This rest might yet have balmed thy broken sinews,'

have been needlessly disturbed by Theobald's con-
jectural emendation ' broken senses.' The metaphor taken from the snapping of a sinew, for which,
more than other bodily hurts, complete rest is the
indispensable cure, is peculiarly expressive here.

Shakespeare is proverbially careless of ana-
chronisms, and in general of what may be called
historical and geographical realism. Yet it is not
less certain that whole plays are coloured more or
less by his conception of the characteristics of a

nation, or the spirit of an age. Now in ' Lear ' and
' Cymbeline' his imagination was carried back under
the guidance of Holinshed to pre-Christian times in
Britain. In ' Lear,' especially, we have an approach
to the Aeschylean notion of an age of moral chaos
or inchoate morality, ' ere humane statute purged the
gentle weal,' an age in which the great elemental
passions had more scope than in more settled times,
and could be let loose by the dramatist with less
improbability. There are not wanting traces in
both dramas of the mode in which Shakespeare
imagined the religion of such a primitive time.
Belarius and his youths bowing at the exit of their
cavern, with the simple worship of ' hail Heaven,'
Imogen's ' orisons' for him she loves, 'at the sixth
hour of morn, at noon, at midnight,' her simple
prayer at going to rest,

> ' To your protection I commend me, gods ;
> From fairies, and the tempters of the night,
> Guard me, beseech ye ! '

are all conceived in the spirit of such an idea.

The touches of this kind in ' Lear ' are more
frequent and slightly more elaborate.   In the
absence of directly Christian notions there is a
deep pervading sense of the mystery of Nature.
Apollo and Hecate—even all-judging Jove—convey
no Greek or Roman associations ; they merely accentuate the general effect of heathenism. To the

ear of Nature Lear addresses his terrible curse;
to Nature Edmund appeals from 'the plague of
custom,' 'the curiosity of nations.' The sun, the
night, the elements, the stellèd fires are easily
personified and play a prominent part in men's
imaginations. 'The gods' in vague plurality occur
more frequently in 'Lear' and 'Cymbeline' than
in any other plays except those whose subject is
distinctly Greek or Roman. The same use occurs,
but less frequently, also in 'The Winter's Tale.'

While Christian beliefs are thus abstracted from,
essentially Pagan fancies respecting malevolent or
mischievous powers are, without scruple, transferred from the Elizabethan to the primitive age.
Gloucester, like Imogen, believes in fairies (IV. vi.
30 ff.), and Edgar is perfect in fiend lore. All kinds
of superstition are supposed to have extraordinary
strength. Gloucester's credulity about eclipses and
the like is despised by Edmund, but the dread of
a father's curse, with all but Goneril, is found sur-
viving even natural affection. Lastly, the belief
in magic is imagined as having a powerful hold,
especially on the eager, unsatisfied mind of Lear.
The search for hidden causes is represented as
having a fascination proportionate to men's ignorance, a tendency which appears in various phases,
from Lear's mad questioning of his 'philosopher'
(whose appearance has taught him the vanity of

' sophistication '), to the touching faith displayed by Cordelia:

> ' All blessed secrets,
> All you unpublished virtues of the earth,
> Spring with my tears ! be aidant and remediate
> In the good man's distress.'

This conception of a heathen past is not consistently carried out ; but there is a sufficient dash of it to add greatly to dramatic illusion.

CHAPTER XVI

'CYMBELINE,' 'WINTER'S TALE,' AND 'TEMPEST'

Romantic plays—Common characteristics—'The Tempest' examined.

OF the three plays which were probably composed after the poet's retirement to Stratford, the editors of the folio placed 'Cymbeline' among the tragedies, and 'The Winter's Tale' as well as 'The Tempest' among the comedies. All three are better grouped together as 'romantic plays,' or, in Dryden's phrase, as belonging to that weaker sort of tragedy which has a happy ending: for in all of them there is a serious intention, and at the same time a large element that does not consort with tragedy. Some mellowing of the poet's mood seems in this to have coincided with a certain 'weakening of the theatre' which is elsewhere apparent in the Jacobean age, but the genius of Shakespeare still reaches far beyond that of his contemporaries.

(1) These plays all conclude with an atonement, with reconciliation. Not only does good triumph over evil, but the persons in whom the evil had been active are brought to a better mind. Leonatus is

overwhelmed with penitence, and, with his happiness restored, Alonzo is told not to burden his remembrance with a heaviness 'that's gone'; even Caliban will sue for grace, and Antonio and Sebastian are included in the general amnesty. Where can be found nobler expressions of the grace of forgiveness than that of Posthumus to Iachimo?

> 'The power that I have on you is to spare you;
> The malice towards you to forgive you; live,
> And deal with others better';

and this of Prospero:

> 'They being penitent,
> The sole drift of my purpose doth extend
> Not a frown further.'

(2) In each of them there is an ideal of feminine purity surpassing even Shakespeare's highest flights elsewhere—Imogen, the perfect wife; Hermione, patient under wrong; Perdita and Miranda, virginal, fearless, impeccable. And if, as seems possible, Shakespeare's contribution to 'Pericles' belongs to the same period, Marina is a worthy member of the flawless sisterhood.

(3) In each there is a strong element of the romantic pastoral. In 'Winter's Tale' the episode of the shepherds' feast; in 'Cymbeline' the idyll of Milford Haven, the cave scenes between the disguised Imogen and Belarius with his two princely boys; in 'The Tempest' the romance of the desert island.

In point of construction, while 'The Tempest' is

perhaps the most faultless of the comedies, 'The Winter's Tale' and 'Cymbeline' come far short of the great tragedies. The truth about them probably lies somewhere between Mr. Richard Moulton's elaborate schematism and the view of Matthew Arnold, who spoke of 'Cymbeline' as 'an impossible broken-backed sort of thing.'

To expatiate on the Romantic Plays would be to wander from 'Tragic Drama'; but a few words on 'The Tempest' may not inaptly conclude this rambling volume.

Rosalind's 'magician profound in his art but not damnable' was a character hardly known to the vulgar of Shakespeare's time. Their simple view of the matter is best reflected in that wonderful fifth act of Marlowe's 'Dr. Faustus,' which for direct intensity of spiritual agony is hardly equalled even by Shakespeare's Clarence or Claudio. But the more enlightened seem to have formed the conception of a sort of white magic, akin to astrology and alchemy, both favourite subjects of allusion with Elizabethan poets; which, as in Paracelsus and Roger Bacon, combined the dignity of science with the glamour and mystery of the supernatural. And in this notion Shakespeare at forty-five saw his opportunity for embodying a more distant and ideal survey of the life in which his art had hitherto been plunged. The feeling of the work resembles that of Goethe's dedication of his 'Faust':

' Ye bring with you the former days of glory,
     Many dear shadows rise to light again ;
They waken, like a scarce remembered story,
     First love and friendship, and revive the pain.

    .   .   .   .   .   .

' I am seized with a long since unwonted yearning
     Toward yonder grave untroubled spirit choir,
My stammering song, as some new language learning,
     Trembles and quavers, like the Aeolian lyre.

    .   .   .   .   .   .

' What I possess, I see afar remote,
And what has vanished—that is real, I wot.'

This deeper motive, and the growing influence of
travellers' tales (especially since the discovery of
Bermuda), together with the altered versification,
distinguish ' The Tempest ' from the comedy which
a kindred subject-matter tempts one to couple with
it, the ' Midsummer Night's Dream.' And it is
obviously no less widely separated from the tragedies
and history plays. Those milder and more harmonious views of life which grow as contemplation
succeeds to action, those ideas of restoration, restitu-
tion, rehabilitation, and also of the harmony of man
with Nature and of the eternal charm of infancy and
early youth—which push their way amidst alien
elements in ' The Winter's Tale ' and ' Cymbeline,'
and in the Shakespearian scenes of ' Pericles '—are
here expressed with consummate purity. And as
was natural in an ideal writing, they are confronted
with their extreme opposites, but so that the evil
is finally overcome by the good—and that not
conventionally but in a manner profoundly real. In

one case, indeed, the dramatic contrast is so vivid as
to betray the superficial reader into a disproportionate
estimate.

As Portia and Shylock are contrasted in the
drama of human friendship, so here the beneficent
and the mischievous agencies which were combined
in Puck are parted between Ariel and Caliban. And
just as Shylock, from vividness of portraiture, is apt
to absorb undue attention, so Caliban, that wonderful
creation, is often dwelt upon more than he deserves.
I will only notice here that his ideal nature is
cunningly indicated by his speaking always in verse,
so that Jaques would have said ' good-bye ' to him.
In ' The Tempest ' the poet is for once consciously
refining upon Nature. But he is still true to his
great principle that

> ' Nature is made better by no mean
> But Nature makes that mean,'

and his most sovereign alchemy consists in drawing
forth the most intimate and familiar secrets of the
heart.

Except in sinning and repenting, Miranda is
much more akin to us than Milton's Eve. Even in
Caliban there are features of the real savage marvel-
lously divined, which, as the Archbishop says of
Prince Hal's theology, ' 'tis a marvel how his grace
should glean them.'

The contrast between Caliban and Trinculo,

mutatis mutandis, recalls Professor Huxley's preference of the Papuan to the East Londoner.

In closing this brief section on a fascinating and
inexhaustible theme, let me call attention to a very
few of these 'touches of Nature' by which that
which seems fantastic at first sight vindicates the
right to be recognised and loved as human.

(1) Prospero, whom the other persons regard
with awe, as a necromancer, has all the partiality of
a father, and is so absorbed in the happiness of his
child that he forgets, not only the enemies whom he
has overthrown, but his present imminent danger
from the attempt of Caliban. What can be more
human than the confession ' A turn or two I'll walk,
to still my beating mind ' ?

(2) When reminded of the situation, he is
horror-stricken—but that which works him to such
unwonted passion is less the peril to himself, than
the obstinate ingratitude of the demi-devil to whom
he has taught so much.

(3) Note also that from his past experience of
the world he underrates the reverential chivalry of
first and passionate love in its earliest stage, and is
over-anxious where Ferdinand is possibly over-con-
fident.

(4) Miranda for the first time breaks her father's
behest in telling her name, and says to Ferdinand,
' He's safe for these three hours.' These are the

blenches at which 'Jove laughs,' and without which
the passion which leads to the forsaking of father
and mother would not be itself. How much she
learns of herself, and of life and conduct, in that
short interview !

(5) Even Ariel, the 'airy spirit' of Titania's
imagination, who has no human feeling (none but
the longing to be free), is aware that lovers would
be alone, and tells Prospero that if he now beheld
his enemies, his affections would become tender
—'Mine would, sir, were I human.'

(6) And even Caliban is not without pathetic
traits. Unacquainted with man, he is familiar after
his fashion with the spirit-world, at least with its
noises and other less agreeable operations, and also
with 'The blind but quick-eared mole, the nimble
marmozet and scamels of the rock'—herein being
more learned than Shakespearian commentators.
His perceptions within their narrow range (even his
ear for music) are true. He knows where the quick
freshes are—the barren place and fertile, and is not
insensible to kindness, though ignorant how it
should be repaid. He has lost his savage liberty by
the advent of civilised man, and though he is conscious of the moral ascendency of Prospero merely
as a stronger witchcraft, in one who is wrapped
up in his books, without which 'he is but a sot as
I am,' yet in the end he too learns his lesson, 'to be
wise and seek for grace.' Nay, Caliban, too, has his

idealisms, and in his dreams sees riches ready to drop on him from the clouds, and his intellectual pride is hurt at the idea of being transformed to an ape ' with forehead villainous low.'

(7) Lastly, the certainty of retribution, ' delaying not forgetting,' and the griping sense of guilt, ' Like poison given to work a great time after,' are not less profoundly true than the noble exercise of power in clemency, which, the moment faults are acknowledged, will press the advantage ' not a frown further.'

The personal application of all this to Shakespeare himself, who in retiring to New Place is supposed to have broken his magic wand, a fancy which Thomas Campbell first made popular, must I fear be classed with other fancies which are more attractive than substantial.[1] Yet it is not unnatural to feel that here more than in any other play we are brought near to the man Shakespeare and overhear his thoughts :

' Thought-wafted to wise Prospero's magic isle
(Once " the wild winds " his art calls forth are " whist ")
We gaze enraptured, pondering as we list
The forms that, mirrored yonder, frown or smile.

---

[1] Mr. Hunter's suggestion of an early date for *The Tempest*, which Mr. Courthope strangely endorses, rests on the allusion in Ben Jonson's prologue to *Every Man in His Humour*. But the prologue is absent from the Quarto of 1601, and the parallel passage in Chapman's *Epicedie* (1612) is more to the point. The exact date of *The Tempest* matters little, so long as it counts with the latest group. The title *Love's Labour's Won* is much more suitable to *All's Well*.

Far off the spell-doomed world, withdrawn the while,
Looms like a dim-seen land through dazzling mist,
And lips like those our childhood-fancy kissed
With air-bred harmonies the spirit beguile.
The charm dissolves; we linger—till a breeze,
No " Tempest " now, a peace-attempered gale,
Risen all unwist, bears us on bright smooth seas
Back to the world, with steadied course to sail
Freighted with wisdom, patience and heartsease,
A treasure that with years shall more prevail.'

INDEX